# FUTURE INTRO

## English for Work, Life, and Academic Success

Second Edition

Series Consultants
**Sarah Lynn**
**Ronna Magy**
**Federico Salas-Isnardi**

Authors
Yvonne Wong Nishio
with Jamie Greene,
Hilary Hodge,
Jessica Miller-Smith,
and Julie Schmidt

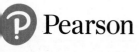

**Pearson**

*Future Intro*
*English for Work, Life, and Academic Success*
Copyright © 2021 by Pearson Education, Inc.

Pearson Education, 221 River Street, Hoboken, NJ 07030 USA

**Staff credits:** The people who made up the *Future* team, representing content development, design, manufacturing, marketing, multimedia, project management, publishing, rights management, and testing, are Pietro Alongi, Jennifer Castro, Dave Dickey, Gina DiLillo, Warren Fischbach, Pamela Fishman, Gosia Jaros-White, Joanna Konieczna, Michael Mone, Mary Perrotta Rich, Katarzyna Starzyńska-Kościuszko, Claire Van Poperin, Joseph Vella, Gabby Wu

**Text composition:** ElectraGraphics, Inc.
**Cover Design:** EMC Design Ltd
**Illustration credits:** See Credits page 249.
**Photo credits:** See Credits page 249.
**Audio:** CityVox
**Development:** Blue Crab Editorial Services

**Library of Congress Cataloging-in-Publication Data**
A catalog record for the print edition is available from the Library of Congress.

ISBN-13: 9780137359240 (Student Book with App and MyEnglishLab)
ISBN-10: 0137359240 (Student Book with App and MyEnglishLab)

ISBN-13: 9780137360307 (Student Book with App)
ISBN-10: 0137360304 (Student Book with App)

Printed in the United States of America
11  2023

pearsonenglish.com

## Welcome to *Future: English for Work, Life, and Academic Success*

*Future* is a six-level, standards-based English language course for adult and young adult students. *Future* provides students with the contextualized academic language, strategies, and critical-thinking skills needed for success in workplace, life, and academic settings. *Future* is aligned with the requirements of the Workforce Innovation and Opportunity Act (WIOA), the English Language Proficiency (ELP) and College and Career Readiness (CCR) standards, and the National Reporting System (NRS) level descriptors. The 21st century curriculum in *Future*'s second edition helps students acquire the basic literacy, language, and employability skills needed to meet the requirements set by the standards.

*Future* develops students' academic and critical thinking skills, digital literacy and numeracy, and workplace and civic skills, and it prepares students for taking standardized tests. Competency and skills incorporating standards are in the curriculum at every level, providing a foundation for academic rigor, research-based teaching strategies, corpus-informed language, and the best of digital tools.

In revising the course, we listened to hundreds of *Future* teachers and learners and studied the standards for guidance. *Future* continues to be the most comprehensive English communication course for adults, with its signature scaffolded lessons and multiple practice activities throughout. *Future*'s second edition provides enhanced content, rigorous academic language practice, and cooperative learning through individual and collaborative practice. Every lesson teaches the interpretive, interactive, and productive skills highlighted in the standards.

### *Future*'s Instructional Design

#### Learner Centered and Outcome Oriented

The student is at the center of *Future*. Lessons start by connecting to student experience and knowledge, and then present targeted skills in meaningful contexts. Varied and dynamic skill practice progresses from controlled to independent in a meticulously scaffolded sequence.

Headers highlighting Depth of Knowledge (DOK) terms are used throughout levels 1–4 of *Future* to illuminate the skills being practiced. Every lesson culminates in an activity in which students apply their learning, demonstrate their knowledge, and express themselves orally or in writing. A DOK glossary for teachers includes specific suggestions on how to help students activate these cognitive skills.

#### Varied Practice

Cognitive science has proven what *Future* always knew: Students learn new skills through varied practice over time. Content-rich units that contextualize academic and employability skills naturally recycle concepts, language, and targeted skills. Individual and collaborative practice activities engage learners and lead to lasting outcomes. Lessons support both student collaboration and individual self-mastery. Students develop the interpretative, productive, and interactive skills identified in the NRS guidelines, while using the four language skills of reading, writing, listening, and speaking.

#### Goal Setting and Learning Assessment

For optimal learning to take place, students need to be involved in setting goals and in monitoring their own progress. *Future* addresses goal setting in numerous ways. In the Student Book, Unit Goals are identified on the unit opener page. Checkboxes at the end of lessons invite students to evaluate their mastery of the material, and suggest additional online practice.

High-quality assessment aligned to the standards checks student progress and helps students prepare to take standardized tests. The course-based assessment program is available in print and digital formats and includes a bank of customizable test items. Digital tests are assigned by the teacher and reported back in the LMS online gradebook. All levels include a midterm and final test. Test items are aligned with unit learning objectives and standards. The course Placement Test is available in print and digital formats. Test-prep materials are also provided for specific standardized tests.

### One Integrated Program

*Future* provides everything adult English language learners need in one integrated program using the latest digital tools and time-tested print resources.

#### Integrated Skills Contextualized with Rich Content

*Future* contextualizes grammar, listening, speaking, pronunciation, reading, writing, and vocabulary in meaningful activities that simulate real workplace, educational, and community settings. A special lesson at the end of each unit highlights soft skills at work. While providing relevant content, *Future* helps build learner knowledge and equips adults for their many roles.

#### Meeting Work, Life, and Education Goals

*Future* recognizes that every adult learner brings a unique set of work, life, and academic experiences, as well as a distinct skill set. With its diverse array of print and digital resources, *Future* provides learners with multiple opportunities to practice with contextualized materials to build skill mastery. Specialized lessons for academic and workplace skill development are part of *Future*'s broad array of print and digital resources.

Every unit of *Future*'s *Intro* level contains a Life Skills lesson as well as an English at Work lesson.

## Life Skills Lessons

In the second edition, the Life Skills lessons in *Future Intro* continue to provide outstanding coverage of life-skills competencies, basing language teaching on real-life situations that students are likely to encounter and focusing on developing the language and civic-literacy skills required today. In addition, every lesson includes practice with digital skills on a mobile device.

## English at Work Lessons

*Future Intro* has further enhanced its development of workplace skills by adding an English at Work lesson to each unit. This new lesson aims to equip students with the critical interpersonal communication skills needed to succeed in any workplace. Students begin each lesson by completing a model conversation with key words and phrases. Then they work collaboratively to practice similar conversations with new information.

## Academic Rigor

Rigor and respect for the ability and experiences of the adult learner have always been central to *Future*. The standards provide the foundation for academic rigor. The reading, writing, listening, and speaking practice requires learners to analyze, use context clues, interpret, cite evidence, build knowledge, support a claim, and summarize from a variety of text formats. Regular practice with complex and content-rich materials develops academic language and builds knowledge. Interactive activities allow for collaboration and exchange of ideas in workplace and academic contexts. *Future* emphasizes rigor by highlighting the critical thinking and problem-solving skills required in each activity.

## Reading and Writing

All reading lessons have engaging stories with cross-cultural topics that are interesting and relevant to students' lives. The information-rich texts are further supported by beautiful illustrations that present stories in graphic novel format.

To further strengthen its academic rigor, *Future Intro* has also increased its focus on writing in Show What You Know! activities. With the focus on integrated skills in mind, reading and writing skills are practiced throughout each unit along with the other skills in a highly contextualized way.

## *Future* Grows with Your Student

*Future* takes learners from absolute beginner level through low-advanced English proficiency, addressing students' abilities and learning priorities at each level. As the levels progress, the curricular content and unit structure change accordingly, with the upper levels incorporating more advanced academic language and skills in the text and in the readings.

| Future Intro | Future Level 1 | Future Level 2 | Future Level 3 | Future Level 4 | Future Advanced |
|---|---|---|---|---|---|
| NRS Beginning ESL Literacy | NRS Low Beginning ESL | NRS High Beginning ESL | NRS Low Intermediate ESL | NRS High Intermediate ESL | NRS Advanced ESL |
| **ELPS** Level 1 | **ELPS** Level 1 | **ELPS** Level 2 | **ELPS** Level 3 | **ELPS** Level 4 | **ELPS** Level 5 |
| **CCRS** Level A | **CCRS** Level A | **CCRS** Level A | **CCRS** Level B | **CCRS** Level C | **CCRS** Level D |
| **CASAS** 180 and below | **CASAS** 181–190 | **CASAS** 191–200 | **CASAS** 201–210 | **CASAS** 211–220 | **CASAS** 221–235 |

The **Pearson Practice English App** provides easy mobile access to all of the audio files, plus Grammar Coach videos and activities, and the new Pronunciation Coach videos. Listen and study on the go—anywhere, any time!

## Abundant Opportunities for Student Practice

**Student**

**Student's Book** is a complete student resource, including lessons in grammar, listening and speaking, pronunciation, reading, writing, vocabulary, and English at Work, taught and practiced in contextual and interactive activities in the eBook.

**Online Practice** allows online independent self-study and interactive practice in pronunciation, grammar, vocabulary, reading, writing, and listening. The portal includes the popular Grammar Coach videos and new Pronunciation Coach videos and activities.

**Workbook**—with audio—provides additional practice for each lesson in the Student Book, with new readings and practice in writing, grammar, listening, and speaking, plus activities for new English at Work lessons.

---

The **Teacher's Edition** includes culture notes, teaching tips, and numerous optional and extension activities, with lesson-by-lesson correlations to CCR and ELP standards. Rubrics are provided for evaluation of students' written and oral communication.

## Outstanding Teacher Resources

**Teacher**

**Presentation tool** for front-of-classroom projection of the Student Book, includes audio at point of use and pop-up activities, including grammar examples, academic conversation stems, and reader's anticipation guide.

**Multilevel Communicative Activities** provide an array of reproducible communication activities and games that engage students through different modalities. Teachers' notes provide multilevel options for pre-level and above-level students, as well as extension activities for additional speaking and writing practice.

**Assessment Program**, accessed online with interactive and printable tests and rubrics, includes a Placement Test; multi-level unit, midterm, and final exams; and computer-based Test Generator with additional ready-to-use and customizable tests. In addition, sample high-stakes test practice is included with CASAS test prep for listening and reading.

---

Go to the Teacher's Portal for easy reference, correlations to federal and state standards, and course updates.
pearsonenglish.com

**Preview** questions activate student background knowledge and help the teacher assess how much students know about the unit theme.

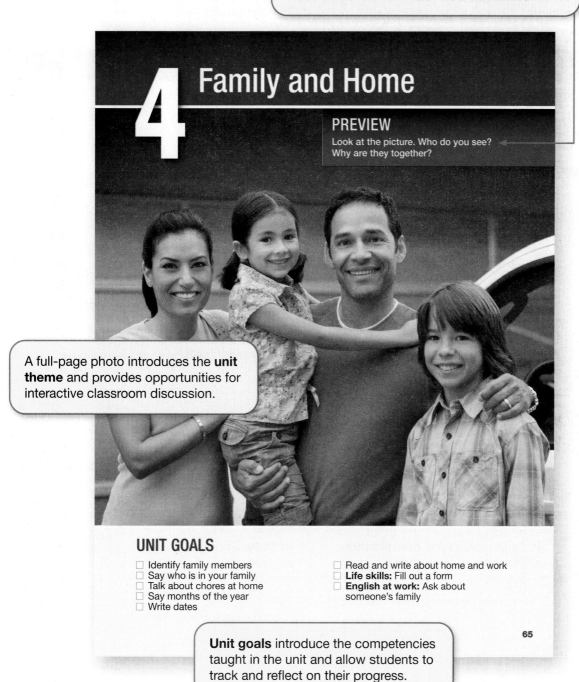

## 4 Family and Home

### PREVIEW

Look at the picture. Who do you see?
Why are they together?

A full-page photo introduces the **unit theme** and provides opportunities for interactive classroom discussion.

### UNIT GOALS

- ☐ Identify family members
- ☐ Say who is in your family
- ☐ Talk about chores at home
- ☐ Say months of the year
- ☐ Write dates

- ☐ Read and write about home and work
- ☐ **Life skills:** Fill out a form
- ☐ **English at work:** Ask about someone's family

65

**Unit goals** introduce the competencies taught in the unit and allow students to track and reflect on their progress.

Key **vocabulary** is contextualized and practiced in connection to the unit theme.

Model **conversations** present the core competency and language of the lesson.

## Identify Family Members

Lesson 1

### That's my brother.

**1 VOCABULARY: Family members**

Ⓐ Look at the pictures. What do you see?

▶ Listen and point. Listen and repeat.

Ⓑ ▶ Listen and read. Listen and repeat.

| 1. sister | 2. brother | 3. husband | 4. wife |
| 5. grandmother | 6. grandfather | 7. parents | 8. father |
| 9. mother | 10. daughter | 11. son | 12. children |

## Identify Family Members

**2 CONVERSATION**

Ⓐ ▶ Listen. Listen and repeat.

A: Who's that?
B: That's my brother.
A: What's his name?
B: Sam.
A: Who's that?
B: That's my sister.
A: What's her name?
B: Her name is Tina.

Ⓑ Practice the conversation.

### Show what you know!

**1. TALK ABOUT IT.** Show pictures of your family. Ask and answer.

A: Who's that?
B: That's my _____.
A: What's _____ name?
B: _____ name is _____.

**2. WRITE ABOUT IT.** Write the names of your family members.

My sister is Emma.
My mother is Angela.

I can identify family members. ■                    I need more practice. ■

Students practice the **conversation** utilizing new **vocabulary** learned in the lesson.

In **Show what you know!**, students apply the target vocabulary in meaningful conversations and in writing.

> **Grammar** is presented in context in model **conversations**.

> **Grammar charts** present the target grammar point in a clear and simple format, providing examples related to the conversation.

## Lesson 2 — Say Who Is in Your Family
### I have two sisters and one brother.

**1 CONVERSATION**

**A** ▶ Listen. Listen and repeat.

**A:** Do you have any sisters or brothers?
**B:** Yes. I have two sisters and one brother.
**A:** That's nice. Do you have any children?
**B:** No, I don't.

**B** Circle *Yes* or *No*.

1. The woman has two sisters.     Yes   No
2. The woman has two brothers.     Yes   No
3. The woman has children.     Yes   No

**C** Practice the conversation.

**2 READING**

**A** ▶ Listen and read.

Hi, I'm Marta. This is my family. That's my husband. His name is Pedro. My parents are Linda and Roberto. I have two sons, Ernesto and Tino. I have one daughter. Her name is Ana.

Pedro   Marta   Linda   Roberto

Tino   Ernesto   Ana

**B** Complete the sentences about Marta's family.

1. Pedro is her _____.
2. Ana is her _____.
3. Linda is her _____.
4. Ernesto and Tino are her _____.
5. Roberto and Linda are her _____.

---

### Say Who Is in Your Family

**3 GRAMMAR: Singular and plural**

**A** ▶ Listen and read. Listen and repeat.

| Singular | Plural |
|---|---|
| one brother | two brothers |
| a sister | three sisters |
| one son | two sons |
| a daughter | three daughters |
| one parent | two parents |
| one child | two children |

**B** Match.

<u>b</u> **1.** my brother Tom and my brother Mark    **a.** my parents
___ **2.** my son and daughter    **b.** my brothers
___ **3.** my mother and father    **c.** my sisters
___ **4.** my sister Sue and my sister Mary    **d.** my children

---

### Show what you know!

**1. TALK ABOUT IT.** Ask and answer.

A: Do you have any sisters or brothers?
B: _____
A: Do you have any children?
B: _____

**2. WRITE ABOUT IT.** Write sentences.

I have one brother.
I have two daughters.

I can say who is in my family. ■      I need more practice. ■

> Target **grammar** is further contextualized in a **reading** passage.

> **Show what you know!** integrates an interactive exchange and a writing task so students demonstrate their mastery of the grammar point using a range of language skills.

**Life Skills** lessons focus on functional language and practical skills. By introducing real-life materials, such as personal forms, they help students to develop document literacy and civic-literacy skills.

**Writing** activities incorporate language from the unit. Students then work collaboratively to practice life skills.

---

Lesson **6** — Life Skills: Fill Out a Form

## What is your teacher's name?

### 1 READING

**A** ▶ Listen and read.

**Adult Education Center**

| Name | | | Today's Date |
|---|---|---|---|
| Viktor | Oleg | Popov | 10/21/2019 |
| First | Middle | Last | |
| Date of Birth | Place of Birth | Class | Teacher |
| 10/30/1994 | Russia | ESL-3 | Mrs. Brown |
| Class Schedule | | | |
| Monday, Wednesday | 2:30–5:30 | | 14 |
| Day/s | Time | | Room |

date of birth: 2/18/2019

**B** Complete the sentences about Viktor.

1. Viktor is a _____.
2. Viktor's last name is _____.
3. He is from _____.
4. Viktor's date of birth is _____.
5. His teacher is _____.
6. His class is _____.
7. His class is on Monday and _____.
8. His class is over at _____.

---

Life Skills: Fill Out a Form

### 2 WRITING

**A** Answer the questions.

1. What is your first name? _____
2. What is your last name? _____
3. What is your date of birth? _____
4. Where are you from? _____
5. What class are you in? _____
6. What is your teacher's name? _____
7. What day is your class? _____
8. What time does your class start? _____
9. What time does your class end? _____
10. What room is your class in? _____

**B** Fill out the form. Use your information in Exercise A.

**Adult Education Center**

| Name | | | Today's Date |
|---|---|---|---|
| First | Middle | Last | |
| Date of Birth | Place of Birth | Class | Teacher |
| Class Schedule | | | |
| Day/s | Time | | Room |

**C** **WORK TOGETHER.** Read your classmate's form. Is the form complete?

**D** GO ONLINE.

1. Find an application form online.
2. Fill out the form.

I can fill out a form. ■    I need more practice. ■

---

**Reading comprehension** questions check students' understanding of the context and vocabulary.

In **Go Online** activities, students use their devices to practice concrete online tasks.

**Checkpoints** at the end of lessons provide students an opportunity to reflect on their progress and identify further resources for more practice.

## Lesson 7 — Read and Write About Home and Work

### Lucas and Carla are married.

#### 1 LISTENING

**A** ▶ Look at each picture. What do you see?

**B** ▶ Listen to the story.

### Read and Write About Home and Work

#### 2 READING

**A** ▶ Read and listen.

> Lucas and Carla are married. Lucas is Carla's husband. Carla is Lucas's wife.
> In their native country, men go to work.
> In their native country, women do the household chores.
> In the United States, Carla and Lucas go to work.
> They both do household chores. Lucas washes the dishes.
> Lucas goes to the supermarket, too.

**B** Circle *Yes* or *No*.

| | | |
|---|---|---|
| 1. Lucas is Carla's husband. | Yes | No |
| 2. In the United States, Carla goes to work. | Yes | No |
| 3. In their native country, women go to work. | Yes | No |
| 4. In the United States, Lucas does household chores. | Yes | No |

#### 3 WRITING

**A** MAKE CONNECTIONS. Talk about work and household chores in your native country.

1. Do men and women go to work?
2. Do women do household chores?
3. Do men do household chores? What household chores do they do?

**B** Complete the sentences.

1. In my native country, _____ work.
2. _____ do household chores.
3. In the United States, _____ work.
4. _____ do household chores.

**C** WORK TOGETHER. Read your sentences.

I can read and write about home and work. ■          I need more practice. ■

New **English at Work** lessons engage students in real-life situations that develop the personal, social, and cultural skills critical for career success, and help students meet the WIOA requirements.

## Lesson 8

### English at Work: Ask About Someone's Family

### Mara is at work.

Mara

Co-worker

### 1 READING

Mara is an assistant.
She works in an office.
She asks her co-worker about her family.

A brief scenario introduces the **character** and the **context** of the conversation.

### 2 CONVERSATION AT WORK

Ⓐ Complete the conversation. Write the correct words.

**Mara:** Is that your family?

**Co-worker:** Yes, it is. That's my _____ and three sisters.

| brother | sister |
|---------|--------|

**Mara:** _____?

| That's nice | Who's that |
|-------------|------------|

**Co-worker:** That's my _____.

| grandmother | grandparents |
|-------------|--------------|

**Mara:** You have a nice family.

**Co-worker:** _____!

| You're welcome | Thank you |
|----------------|-----------|

Ⓑ Practice the conversation.

Ⓒ Role-play the conversation with new information.

| I can ask about someone's family. ■ | I need more practice. ■ |
|---|---|

For more practice, go to MyEnglishLab.

Conversation activities are highly scaffolded and progress from controlled to open practice. Students first complete the conversation with key words and phrases. They then proceed to create similar conversations with new information.

> **Review** lessons at the end of each unit provide extra practice for **vocabulary**, **grammar**, **conversation**, **life skills**, and **writing**.

> **Vocabulary Review** includes listening and repeating, categorizing, labeling, and matching exercises.

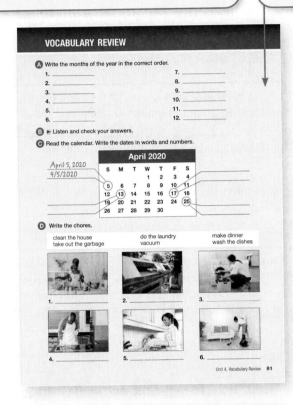

### VOCABULARY REVIEW

**A** Write the months of the year in the correct order.

1. _____    7. _____
2. _____    8. _____
3. _____    9. _____
4. _____    10. _____
5. _____    11. _____
6. _____    12. _____

**B** ▶ Listen and check your answers.

**C** Read the calendar. Write the dates in words and numbers.

April 5, 2020
4/5/2020

**April 2020**

| S | M | T | W | T | F | S |
|---|---|---|---|---|---|---|
|   |   |   | 1 | 2 | 3 | 4 |
| 5 | 6 | 7 | 8 | 9 | 10 | 11 |
| 12 | 13 | 14 | 15 | 16 | 17 | 18 |
| 19 | 20 | 21 | 22 | 23 | 24 | 25 |
| 26 | 27 | 28 | 29 | 30 |   |   |

**D** Write the chores.

clean the house   do the laundry   make dinner
take out the garbage   vacuum   wash the dishes

1. _____   2. _____   3. _____
4. _____   5. _____   6. _____

Unit 4, Vocabulary Review   **81**

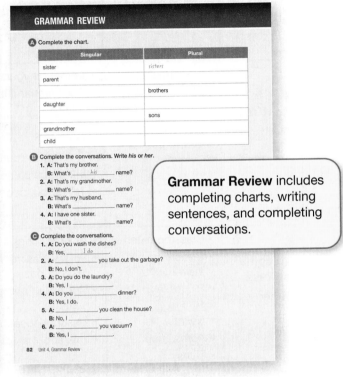

### GRAMMAR REVIEW

**A** Complete the chart.

| Singular | Plural |
|---|---|
| sister | sisters |
| parent |  |
|  | brothers |
| daughter |  |
|  | sons |
| grandmother |  |
| child |  |

**B** Complete the conversations. Write *his* or *her*.
1. A: That's my brother.
   B: What's _____his_____ name?
2. A: That's my grandmother.
   B: What's _____ name?
3. A: That's my husband.
   B: What's _____ name?
4. A: I have one sister.
   B: What's _____ name?

**C** Complete the conversations.
1. A: Do you wash the dishes?
   B: Yes, ___I do___.
2. A: _____ you take out the garbage?
   B: No, I don't.
3. A: Do you do the laundry?
   B: Yes, I _____.
4. A: Do you _____ dinner?
   B: Yes, I do.
5. A: _____ you clean the house?
   B: No, I _____.
6. A: _____ you vacuum?
   B: Yes, I _____.

**82**   Unit 4, Grammar Review

> **Grammar Review** includes completing charts, writing sentences, and completing conversations.

### CONVERSATION REVIEW

**ROLE-PLAY.**

Show pictures of your family. Or talk about this picture.

**Student A**
Ask about Student B's family.

**Student B**
Ask about Student A's family.

A: Who's that?
B: That's my _____.
A: What's _____ name?
B: _____

Unit 4, Conversation Review   **83**

> **Conversation Review** first presents a picture or an illustration that sets the context of the conversation, prompting students' role-play activity that is scaffolded with sentence stems.

### LIFE SKILLS AND WRITING REVIEW

**1** LIFE SKILLS: Fill out a form

Fill out the form.

**Student Information Form**   T L C
The Language Center

○ Mr. ○ Mrs. ○ Miss ○ Ms.
Name     Today's Date

First   Middle   Last
Date of Birth   Place of Birth   Class   Teacher

Class Schedule

Day/s    Time    Room

**2** WRITE ABOUT YOURSELF

Complete the sentences.
1. My name is _____
2. I'm from _____
3. I'm in _____
4. My teacher is _____
5. I go to English class on _____
6. Class starts at _____

Unit Review: Go back to page 65. Which unit goals can you check off?

**84**   Unit 4, Life Skills and Writing Review

> **Life Skills and Writing Review** provides students an opportunity to practice with similar real-life material and the functional language presented in the Life Skills lesson.

| Unit | Vocabulary | Listening and Speaking | Reading | Grammar |
|------|-----------|------------------------|---------|---------|
| **Pre-Unit**<br>**Getting Started**<br>*page 2* | • Activities in the classroom<br>• The alphabet<br>• Numbers 1–10 | • Follow classroom instructions<br>• Understand the alphabet<br>• Understand the numbers | • Locate sections in the book | • Introduction to imperatives |
| **1**<br>**Nice to Meet You**<br>*page 5* | • Countries<br>• The alphabet<br>• Numbers 0–9<br>• *He, she*<br>• *You, we, they* | • Introduce yourself<br>• Spell first and last names<br>• Say important numbers<br>• Talk about yourself<br>• Introduce someone<br>• Talk about people | • Read a form<br>• Read about greetings | • *I am, you are*<br>• *He is, she is*<br>• *You are, we are, they are* |
| **2**<br>**Welcome to Class**<br>*page 27* | • Classroom items<br>• Classroom instructions<br>• Places in a school<br>• *Next to*<br>• *Across from*<br>• Titles<br>• Study skills | • Ask for things in class<br>• Follow classroom instructions<br>• Talk about places in a school<br>• Describe locations<br>• Talk about study skills | • Read an online form<br>• Read about classrooms | • Imperatives<br>• Simple present: *I, you, we, they* |
| **3**<br>**On Time**<br>*page 47* | • Numbers and time<br>• Daily activities<br>• Days of the week | • Say the time<br>• Talk about time and schedules<br>• Talk about daily activities<br>• Talk about your weekly schedule | • Read a weekly schedule<br>• Read about time | • *From / to, at, on* |
| **4**<br>**Family and Home**<br>*page 65* | • Family members<br>• Household chores<br>• Months and seasons<br>• Dates | • Identify family members<br>• Say who is in your family<br>• Talk about chores at home<br>• Say months of the year<br>• Talk about dates | • Read about someone's family members<br>• Read an application form<br>• Read about home and work | • Singular and plural<br>• *Yes / No* questions |

| Writing | Document Literacy Numeracy | Life Skills | English At Work |
|---|---|---|---|
| • Write the alphabet<br>• Write the numbers | • Understand numbers 1–10 | • Introduce yourself<br>• Understand course numbers and room numbers for school | |
| • Write first and last names<br>• Write important numbers<br>• Fill out a form<br>• Write about greetings | • Interpret a world map<br>• Read a student ID<br>• Understand an online form | • Read and fill out a form<br><br>**Digital skill:**<br>• Go online and find your school's website. | • Say hello |
| • Fill out an online form<br>• Write about classrooms | • Interpret a floor map<br>• Understand an online form | • Understand a form<br><br>**Digital skill:**<br>• Find a form online and write your information. | • Help someone fill out a form |
| • Write a weekly schedule<br>• Write about time | • Tell time from a digital clock<br>• Tell time from an analog clock<br>• Interpret daily and weekly schedules | • Read and write a weekly schedule<br><br>**Digital skill:**<br>• Go online and find the class schedule for your school. | • Talk about schedules |
| • Write about home and work | • Interpret a yearly calendar<br>• Understand the format of dates | • Fill out a form<br><br>**Digital skill:**<br>• Find an application form online and fill out the form. | • Ask about someone's family |

Text in purple refers to workplace and employability topics.

# SCOPE AND SEQUENCE

| Unit | Vocabulary | Listening and Speaking | Reading | Grammar |
|------|-----------|------------------------|---------|---------|
| **5**<br>**How Much Is It?**<br>*page 85* | • U.S. coins<br>• U.S. bills<br>• Drugstore items<br>• Prices | • Make change with U.S. coins<br>• Make change with U.S. bills<br>• Ask for and say prices | • Read a receipt<br>• Read about shopping | • *Where is, where are* |
| **6**<br>**Let's Eat**<br>*page 103* | • Vegetables<br>• Fruit<br>• Amounts<br>• Containers<br>• Food on a menu | • Talk about vegetables<br>• Say what you like and don't like<br>• Say what someone likes and doesn't like<br>• Ask what someone needs<br>• Order food at a restaurant | • Read an ad<br>• Read a menu<br>• Read about eating | • *Like, don't like*<br>• *Likes, doesn't like* |
| **7**<br>**Apartment for Rent**<br>*page 123* | • Rooms in a home<br>• Words to describe rooms<br>• Furniture and appliances<br>• Addresses | • Identify rooms in a home<br>• Talk about a home<br>• Ask about furniture and appliances<br>• Give an address | • Read an envelope<br>• Read about moving | • *There is, there are*<br>• *Is there, are there* |
| **8**<br>**Let's Go Shopping**<br>*page 141* | • Clothing<br>• Clothing sizes<br>• Colors<br>• Problems with clothing | • Identify clothing you need<br>• Ask for clothing sizes<br>• Describe clothing<br>• Return clothing to a store | • Read a store ad<br>• Read about clothing at a wedding | • *This, that, these, those*<br>• Adjective + noun |

| Writing | Document Literacy Numeracy | Life Skills | English At Work |
|---|---|---|---|
| • Write about shopping | • Recognize U.S. currency<br>• Understand price tags<br>• Calculate prices<br>• Understand a receipt | • Read a receipt<br><br>**Digital skill:**<br>• Find an online drugstore and add up the total price of several items you want to buy. | • Answer a customer's questions |
| • Write shopping lists<br>• Write about eating | • Understand a supermarket ad<br>• Understand a menu<br>• Understand units of measurement | • Read an ad<br>• Make a shopping list<br><br>**Digital skill:**<br>• Find your favorite supermarket online and write the names and prices of the foods you need to buy. | • Do an inventory |
| • Write about moving | • Interpret a floor map<br>• Understand apartment ads<br>• Understand an envelope | • Address an envelope<br>• Read an ad<br><br>**Digital skill:**<br>• Find a business's address online and address an envelope to the business. | • Talk about apartments |
| • Write about clothing at a wedding | • Interpret store ads | • Read store ads<br><br>**Digital skill:**<br>• Find a sale on a clothing store website and write the information. | • Help a customer return clothes |

Text in purple refers to workplace and employability topics.

| Unit | Vocabulary | Listening and Speaking | Reading | Grammar |
|---|---|---|---|---|
| **9**<br>**Our Busy Lives**<br>*page 159* | • Free-time activities<br>• Activities at home<br>• Workplace activities | • Talk about what you do for fun<br>• Talk about what you are doing<br>• Ask about ongoing activities<br>• Talk about ongoing activities at work | • Read the transcript of a voicemail<br>• Read about weekend schedules | • Present continuous<br>• Present continuous: *Yes / No* questions and answers<br>• Present continuous negative |
| **10**<br>**Where's the Bus Stop?**<br>*page 177* | • Places in the community<br>• Public places<br>• Getting to work<br>• Directions<br>• Traffic signs | • Ask about places in the community<br>• Ask where places are<br>• Ask about transportation<br>• Ask for and give directions | • Read about transportation | • *Between, across from* |
| **11**<br>**Get Well Soon**<br>*page 195* | • The body<br>• Medical instructions<br>• Health problems<br>• Emergencies | • Make an appointment<br>• Listen to a doctor<br>• Offer suggestions<br>• Call 911 for emergencies | • Read a medicine label<br>• Read about a doctor's appointment | • *Should* |
| **12**<br>**What Do You Do?**<br>*page 213* | • Jobs<br>• More jobs<br>• Job skills | • Say your occupation<br>• Ask about someone's job<br>• Talk about job skills<br>• Apply for a job | • Read about a job interview | • *Where do / Where does*<br>• *Can* |

| Writing | Document Literacy Numeracy | Life Skills | English At Work |
|---------|----------------------------|-------------|-----------------|
| • Write about weekend schedules | • Interpret a monthly schedule | • Leave a voicemail<br>• Talk about your schedule<br><br>**Digital skill:**<br>• Use your phone to call a classmate or your teacher and leave a voicemail message. | • Take a personal call |
| • Write about transportation | • Interpret a street map<br>• Recognize traffic signs | • Read traffic signs<br><br>**Digital skill:**<br>• Find more traffic signs online and draw one new sign. | • Give directions |
| • Write about a doctor's appointment | • Understand a medicine label | • Read a medicine label<br><br>**Digital skill:**<br>• Search online for images of medicine labels and write the instructions. | • Help someone make an appointment |
| • Write about a job interview | • Read online job ads | • Read a job ad<br>• Fill out a job application<br><br>**Digital skill:**<br>• Find a job ad online and write the skills you need for the job. | • Apply for a new job |

Text in purple refers to workplace and employability topics.

| Unit | CASAS Reading Standards (correlated to CASAS Reading Standards 2016) | CASAS Listening Standards (correlated to CASAS Listening Basic Skills Content Standards) |
|---|---|---|
| 1 | **L1:** RDG 1.7, 3.4; **L2:** RDG 1.2, 1.7, 1.8; **L3:** RDG 1.4, 1.7, 1.8; **L4:** RDG 1.7, 1.8, 2.10, 3.4; **L5:** RDG 1.7, 2.9, 2.10; **L6:** RDG 1.7, 2.9, 2.10; **L7:** RDG 1.4, 1.7, 1.8, 3.3; **L8:** RDG 1.7, 1.8, 3.2; **L9:** RDG 1.7, 1.8, 3.2 | **L1:** 2.1, 2.3, 4.1, 4.2; **L2:** 2.1, 2.2, 4.1, 4.2; **L3:** 2.1, 4.1, 4.2; **L4:** 2.1, 2.3, 3.3, 4.1, 4.2; **L5:** 2.1, 2.3, 3.1, 3.3, 4.1, 4.2; **L6:** 2.1, 2.3, 3.1, 3.2, 3.3, 4.1, 4.2; **L7:** 2.1, 2.3, 4.2; **L8:** 2.1, 2.3, 4.1, 4.2; **L9:** 2.1, 2.3 |
| 2 | **L1:** RDG 1.7, 1.8, 2.3; **L2:** RDG 1.7, 1.8, 2.10; **L3:** RDG 1.7, 1.8, 2.3; **L4:** RDG 1.7, 1.8, 3.4; **L5:** RDG 1.4, 1.7, 1.8, 3.3; **L6:** RDG 1.7, 2.9, 2.10; **L7:** RDG 1.8, 3.2; **L8:** RDG 1.7, 1.8, 3.2 | **L1:** 2.1, 2.3, 4.1, 4.2; **L2:** 3.4, 4.1, 4.2, 5.4; **L3:** 2.1, 2.3, 4.1, 4.2; **L4:** 2.1, 2.3, 4.1, 4.2; **L5:** 2.1, 4.2; **L6:** 2.1, 2.3, 2.4, 3.1, 3.2, 4.1, 4.2; **L7:** 2.1, 2.4, 4.2; **L8:** 2.1, 2.3, 2.4, 4.1, 4.2 |
| 3 | **L1:** RDG 1.4; **L2:** RDG 1.4, 1.7, 1.8, 2.9, 2.10; **L3:** RDG 1.4, 1.7, 1.8; **L4:** RDG 1.7, 1.8, 3.2; **L5:** RDG 1.4, 1.7, 1.8, 3.2; **L6:** RDG 1.4, 1.7, 1.8, 3.2; **L7:** RDG 1.4, 1.7, 1.8, 3.2 | **L1:** 2.1, 4.2; **L2:** 2.1, 2.3, 4.2; **L3:** 2.1, 2.3, 2.4, 4.1, 4.2; **L4:** 2.4, 3.1, 4.2; **L6:** 2.1, 2.3, 4.1, 4.2; **L7:** 2.1, 2.3, 4.1, 4.2 |
| 4 | **L1:** RDG 1.7, 1.8; **L2:** RDG 1.7, 1.8, 2.10; **L3:** RDG 1.7, 1.8, 2.3, 2.9, 2.10; **L4:** RDG 1.4, 1.7, 1.8, 2.1; **L5:** RDG 1.4, 1.7, 1.8; **L6:** RDG 1.7, 3.3; **L7:** RDG 1.8, 3.2; **L8:** RDG 1.7, 1.8, 3.2 | **L1:** 2.1, 2.3, 4.1, 4.2; **L2:** 3.7, 4.1, 4.2; **L3:** 2.1, 2.3, 3.6, 4.1, 4.2; **L4:** 2.1, 2.3, 4.1, 4.2, 4.3; **L5:** 2.1, 2.3, 4.1, 4.2; **L6:** 2.1, 2.3, 4.2; **L7:** 2.1, 2.4, 4.2; **L8:** 2.1, 2.3, 4.1, 4.2 |
| 5 | **L1:** RDG 1.4, 1.7, 1.8; **L2:** RDG 1.4, 1.7, 1.8; **L3:** RDG 1.7, 1.8; **L4:** RDG 1.4, 1.7, 1.8; **L5:** RDG 1.4, 1.7, 1.8; **L6:** RDG 1.7, 3.2; **L7:** RDG 1.4, 1.7, 1.8, 3.2 | **L1:** 2.1, 2.3, 4.1, 4.2; **L2:** 2.1, 2.3, 4.1, 4.2; **L3:** 2.1, 2.3, 3.6, 4.1, 4.2; **L4:** 2.1, 2.3, 3.6, 4.1, 4.2; **L5:** 2.1, 2.3, 4.1, 4.2; **L6:** 2.1, 2.3, 4.2; **L7:** 2.1, 2.3, 4.1, 4.2 |
| 6 | **L1:** RDG 1.7, 1.8; **L2:** RDG 1.7, 1.8, 2.10; **L3:** RDG 1.7, 1.8, 2.10, 3.2; **L4:** RDG 1.4, 1.7, 1.8; **L5:** RDG 1.4, 1.7, 1.8, 2.1, 2.2; **L6:** RDG 1.4, 1.7; **L7:** RDG 1.8, 3.2; **L8:** RDG 1.7, 1.8, 3.2 | **L1:** 2.1, 2.3, 4.1, 4.2; **L2:** 3.3, 4.1, 4.2, 4.3; **L3:** 3.3, 4.1, 4.2, 4.3; **L4:** 2.1, 2.3, 3.7, 4.1, 4.2, 4.3; **L5:** 2.1, 2.3, 2.4, 4.1, 4.2; **L6:** 2.1, 2.3, 2.4, 4.2; **L7:** 2.1, 2.4, 4.2; **L8:** 2.1, 2.3, 4.1, 4.2, 4.3 |
| 7 | **L1:** RDG 1.7, 1.8, 3.4; **L2:** RDG 1.7, 1.8, 3.4; **L3:** RDG 1.7, 1.8, 2.10, 3.4; **L4:** RDG 1.4, 1.7, 1.8; **L5:** RDG 1.4, 1.7, 1.8, 2.2; **L6:** RDG 1.7, 3.2; **L7:** RDG 1.7, 1.8, 3.2 | **L1:** 2.1, 2.3, 4.1, 4.2; **L2:** 2.1, 2.3, 3.1, 4.1, 4.2; **L3:** 2.1, 2.3, 3.1, 3.3, 4.1, 4.2; **L4:** 2.1, 2.3, 4.1, 4.2; **L6:** 2.1, 2.3, 4.2; **L7:** 2.1, 2.3, 4.1, 4.2 |
| 8 | **L1:** RDG 1.7, 1.8; **L2:** RDG 1.7, 1.8, 2.9, 2.10; **L3:** RDG 1.7, 1.8, 2.9, 2.10; **L4:** RDG 1.7, 1.8; **L5:** RDG 1.4, 1.7, 1.8, 2.2; **L6:** RDG 1.7, 3.2; **L7:** RDG 1.7, 1.8, 3.2 | **L1:** 2.1, 2.3, 4.1, 4.2; **L2:** 2.1, 2.3, 4.1, 4.2; **L3:** 2.1, 2.3, 4.1, 4.2; **L4:** 2.1, 2.3, 4.1, 4.2; **L6:** 2.1, 2.3, 4.1, 4.2; **L7:** 2.1, 2.3, 4.1, 4.2 |
| 9 | **L1:** RDG 1.4, 1.7, 1.8, 3.4; **L2:** RDG 1.7, 1.8, 2.9, 2.10, 3.2; **L3:** RDG 1.7, 1.8, 2.9, 2.10; **L4:** RDG 1.7, 1.8, 2.9, 2.10; **L5:** RDG 1.7, 1.8; **L6:** RDG 1.7, 3.2; **L7:** RDG 1.7, 1.8, 3.2 | **L1:** 2.1, 2.3, 4.1, 4.2; **L2:** 2.1, 2.3, 3.9, 4.1, 4.2; **L3:** 2.1, 2.3, 3.6, 3.9, 4.1, 4.2; **L4:** 2.1, 2.3, 3.9, 4.1, 4.2; **L5:** 2.1, 2.3, 4.2; **L6:** 2.1, 2.3, 4.1, 4.2; **L7:** 2.1, 2.3, 4.1, 4.2 |
| 10 | **L1:** RDG 1.7, 1.8, 3.4; **L2:** RDG 1.7, 1.8, 3.4; **L3:** RDG 1.7, 1.8; **L4:** RDG 1.7, 1.8, 3.4; **L5:** RDG 1.3, 1.7, 1.8; **L6:** RDG 1.7, 1.8, 3.2; **L7:** RDG 1.7, 1.8, 3.2 | **L1:** 2.1, 2.3, 4.1, 4.2; **L2:** 2.1, 2.3, 4.1, 4.2; **L3:** 2.1, 2.3, 4.1, 4.2; **L4:** 2.1, 2.3, 4.1, 4.2; **L5:** 2.1, 2.3, 4.2; **L6:** 2.1, 2.3, 4.1, 4.2; **L7:** 2.1, 2.3, 4.1, 4.2 |
| 11 | **L1:** RDG 1.4, 1.7, 1.8; **L2:** RDG 1.7, 1.8; **L3:** RDG 1.7, 1.8; **L4:** RDG 1.7, 1.8, 3.4; **L5:** RDG 1.3, 1.4, 1.7, 1.8, 2.2; **L6:** RDG 1.7, 1.8, 3.2; **L7:** RDG 1.7, 1.8, 3.2 | **L1:** 2.1, 2.3, 4.1, 4.2; **L2:** 2.1, 2.3, 4.1, 4.2; **L3:** 2.1, 2.3, 4.1, 4.2; **L4:** 2.1, 2.3, 4.1, 4.2; **L5:** 2.1, 2.3, 4.2; **L6:** 2.1, 2.3, 4.1, 4.2; **L7:** 2.1, 2.3, 4.1, 4.2 |
| 12 | **L1:** RDG 1.7, 1.8; **L2:** RDG 1.7, 1.8, 2.9, 2.10; **L3:** RDG 1.7, 1.8; **L4:** RDG 1.7, 1.8, 2.9, 2.10; **L5:** RDG 1.4, 1.7, 1.8; **L6:** RDG 1.7, 1.8, 3.2; **L7:** RDG 1.7, 1.8, 3.2 | **L1:** 2.1, 2.3, 4.1, 4.2; **L2:** 2.1, 2.3, 3.6, 4.1, 4.2; **L3:** 2.1, 2.3, 4.1, 4.2; **L4:** 2.1, 2.3, 3.1, 3.9, 4.1, 4.2; **L5:** 2.1, 2.3, 4.2; **L6:** 2.1, 2.3, 4.1, 4.2; **L7:** 2.1, 2.3, 4.1, 4.2 |

**CASAS:** Comprehensive Adult Student Assessment System
**CCRS:** College and Career Readiness Standards (R=Reading; W=Writing; SL=Speaking/Listening; L=Language)
**ELPS:** English Language Proficiency Standards

| CASAS Competencies (correlated to CASAS Competencies: Essential Life and Work skills for Youth and Adults) | CCRS Correlations, Level A | ELPS Correlations, Level 1 |
|---|---|---|
| **L1:** 0.1.2, 0.1.4, 0.1.5, 0.2.1; **L2:** 0.1.2, 0.1.5, 0.2.1; **L3:** 0.1.2, 0.1.5, 0.2.1; **L4:** 0.1.2, 0.1.5, 0.2.1; **L5:** 0.1.2, 0.1.4, 0.1.5; **L6:** 0.1.2, 0.1.4, 0.1.5; **L7:** 0.1.2, 0.1.5, 0.2.2, 2.8.5; 7.4.4, 7.7.3; **L8:** 0.1.1, 0.1.2, 0.1.4, 0.1.5; **L9:** 0.1.2, 0.1.4, 0.1.5 | **L1:** SL1.1, SL.K.3, L1.5a, L1.5c, L1.6; **L2:** SL1.1, L1.1a; **L4:** SL1.4, SL.K.6, L1.1c, L1.1d, L1.1e, L1.1g, L1.1l; **L5:** SL1.4, SL.K.6, L1.1c, L1.1d, L1.1e, L1.1g, L1.1l; **L6:** SL.1.4, L.1.1c, L.1.1d, L.1.1e, L.1.1g, L.1.1l, L.1.6; **L7:** W.1.7, W.1.8; **L8:** RI/RL.1.1, RI.1.4, RI.1.7, SL.K.2 | ELPS 1–3, 5, 7–9 |
| **L1:** 0.1.2, 0.1.4, 0.1.5, 0.2.1; **L2:** 0.1.5, 0.1.7; **L3:** 0.1.2, 0.1.5; **L4:** 0.1.2, 0.1.5, 2.2.1; **L5:** 0.1.2, 0.1.5, 0.2.2, 2.8.5; 7.4.4, 7.7.3; **L6:** 0.1.2, 0.1.5, 0.2.1, 7.4.1; **L7:** 0.1.2, 0.1.5, 0.2.1, 4.4.3; **L8:** 0.1.2, 0.1.5, 0.2.1 | **L1:** SL.1.4, SL.K.6, L1.5a, L1.5c, L1.6; **L2:** SL.K.3, L.1.1l, L.1.6; **L3:** SL.1.1, SL.K.6, L1.5a, L.1.6; **L4:** SL.1.1, L.1.1j; **L5:** RI/RL.1.1, W.1.7, W.1.8; **L6:** L.1.1e, L.1.1g; **L7:** RI/RL.1.1, RI.1.2, RI.1.3, RI.1.4, RI.1.7, SL.K.2 | ELPS 1–3, 5, 7–10 |
| **L1:** 0.1.2, 0.1.5, 2.3.1; **L2:** 0.1.2, 0.1.5, 2.3.1; **L3:** 0.1.2, 0.1.5, 0.2.1, 2.3.1; **L4:** 0.1.2, 0.1.5, 2.8.3; **L5:** 0.1.2, 0.1.5, 2.8.3, 7.4.4, 7.7.3; **L6:** 0.1.2, 0.1.5; **L7:** 0.1.2, 0.1.4, 0.1.5, 4.6.1 | **L1:** SL.1.1, SL.K.3, SL.K.6, L1.5a, L1.5c, L1.6; **L2:** SL.1.4, L.1.1j, L.1.1l, L.1.6; **L3:** SL.1.1, SL.K.3, SL.K.6, L1.5a, L.1.5c, L.1.6; **L4:** L.1.1j, L.1.2b; **L5:** RI/RL.1.1, RI.1.2, W.1.2, W.1.7, W.1.8, SL.K.2; **L6:** RI/RL.1.1, RI.1.2, RI.1.4, RI.1.7, SL.K.2; **L7:** RI/RL.1.1, RI.1.2, RI.1.3, RI.1.4, RI.1.7, SL.K.2 | ELPS 1–3, 5, 7–10 |
| **L1:** 0.1.2, 0.1.5, 0.2.1; **L2:** 0.1.2, 0.1.5, 0.2.1; **L3:** 0.1.2, 0.1.5; **L4:** 0.1.2, 0.1.5, 0.1.8, 2.3.2; **L5:** 0.1.2, 0.1.4, 0.1.5, 2.3.2; **L6:** 0.1.2, 0.1.5, 0.2.1, 2.8.5, 7.4.4, 7.7.3; **L7:** 0.1.2, 0.1.5, 0.2.1, 7.5.5, 8.2.3; **L8:** 0.1.2, 0.1.4, 0.1.5 | **L1:** SL.K.3, SL.K.6, L.1.6; **L2:** SL.1.1, SL.K.3, L.1.1b, L.1.1c; **L3:** SL.1.1, SL.K.2, L.1.1k, L.1.1l, L.1.2c, L.1.2d, L.1.5c, L.1.6; **L4:** L.1.2b, L.1.5a, L.1.6; **L5:** SL.1.4, SL.K.6 RI/RL.1.1, RI.1.2, W.1.2, W.1.7, W.1.8, SL.K.2; **L6:** RI/RL.1.1, RI.1.2, W.1.7, W.1.8; **L7:** RI/RL.1.1, RI.1.2, RI.1.3, RI.1.4, RI.1.7 | ELPS 1–3, 5, 7–10 |
| **L1:** 0.1.2, 0.1.5, 1.1.6; **L2:** 0.1.2, 0.1.5, 1.1.6; **L3:** 0.1.2, 0.1.5, 1.4.1; **L4:** 0.1.2, 0.1.5, 1.1.6, 1.4.1; **L5:** 0.1.2, 0.1.5, 1.1.6, 1.6.4, 7.4.4, 7.7.3; **L6:** 0.1.2, 0.1.5, 1.2.2; **L7:** 0.1.2, 0.1.4, 0.1.5, 1.1.6 | **L1:** SL.1.4, L.1.6; **L2:** SL.1.1, SL.K.2, L.1.6; **L3:** SL.K.2, SL.K.3, SL.K.6, L.1.1k, L.1.1l, L.1.5a, L.1.5c, L.1.6; **L4:** SL.K.3, SL.K.6; **L5:** RI/RL.1.1, RI.1.2, W.1.7, W.1.8, L.1.5c; **L6:** RI/RL.1.1, RI.1.2, RI.1.3, RI.1.4, RI.1.7; **L7:** RI/RL.1.1, RI.1.2, RI.1.3, RI.1.4, RI.1.7 | ELPS 1–3, 5, 7–10 |
| **L1:** 0.1.2, 0.1.4, 0.1.5, 0.1.6, 1.2.8; **L2:** 0.1.2, 0.1.5, 0.2.1; **L3:** 0.1.2, 0.1.5, 0.2.1; **L4:** 0.1.2, 0.1.5, 1.1.6, 1.2.8; **L5:** 0.1.2, 0.1.5, 1.1.6, 1.2.8, 7.4.4, 7.7.3; **L6:** 0.1.2, 0.1.5, 1.1.6, 0.2.1, 2.6.4; **L7:** 0.1.2, 0.1.5, 2.7.9; **L8:** 0.1.2, 0.1.5 | **L1:** SL.1.1, L.1.5c, L.1.6; **L2:** L.1.1c; **L3:** SL.1.1, SL.K.6, L.1.1c, L.1.1l, L.1.5c, L.1.6; **L4:** SL.K.6, L.1.1c, L.1.5a, L.1.6; **L5:** RI/RL.1.1, RI.1.4, RI.1.7, W.1.7, W.1.8; **L6:** SL.1.4; **L7:** RI/RL.1.1, RI.1.2, RI.1.3, SL.K.2, SL.K.3 | ELPS 1–10 |
| **L1:** 0.1.2, 0.1.5, 1.4.1; **L2:** 0.1.2, 0.1.5, 1.4.1; **L3:** 0.1.2, 0.1.5, 1.4.1; **L4:** 0.1.2, 0.1.5, 1.1.6, 1.4.4, 1.4.2; **L5:** 0.1.2, 0.1.5, 0.2.3, 2.4.1, 7.4.4, 7.7.3; **L6:** 0.1.2, 0.1.4, 0.1.5; **L7:** 0.1.2, 0.1.5, 1.1.6, 1.4.1, 1.4.2 | **L1:** SL.1.4, SL.K.6, L.1.6; **L2:** SL.1.1, SL.K.6, L.1.1l, L.1.6; **L3:** SL.1.1, SL.K.3, L.1.1k, L.1.5a, L.1.5c; **L5:** RI/RL.1.1, RI.1.4, W.1.7, W.1.8; **L6:** RI/RL.1.1, RI.1.2, RI.1.3, SL.K.2, SL.K.3; **L7:** RI/RL.1.1, RI.1.2, RI.1.3, RI.1.7, SL.K.2, SL.K.3 | ELPS 1–3, 5, 7–10 |
| **L1:** 0.1.2, 0.1.5, 1.2.9; **L2:** 0.1.2, 0.1.4, 0.1.5, 1.2.9; **L3:** 0.1.2, 0.1.4, 0.1.5, 1.2.9; **L4:** 0.1.2, 0.1.5, 1.2.9, 1.3.3; **L5:** 0.1.2, 0.1.5, 1.2.2, 1.2.9, 7.4.4, 7.7.3; **L6:** 0.1.2, 0.1.5, 1.2.9, 2.7.2, 2.7.9; **L7:** 0.1.2, 0.1.4, 0.1.5, 1.3.3 | **L1:** SL.1.1, SL.K.3, L.1.5c, L.1.6; **L2:** SL.1.1, SL.K.6, L.1.6; **L3:** SL.K.3, SL.1.4, SL.K.6, L.1.1b, L.1.1f, L.1.1g, L.1.1l, L.1.5c; **L4:** L.1.6; **L5:** RI/RL.1.1, RI.1.4, RI.1.7, W.1.7, W.1.8, SL.K.2; **L6:** RI/RL.1.1, RI.1.2, RI.1.3, RI.1.7, SL.K.2 | ELPS 1–3, 7–10 |
| **L1:** 0.1.2, 0.1.5, 0.2.4; **L2:** 0.1.2, 0.1.4, 0.1.5, 0.2.4; **L3:** 0.1.2, 0.1.4, 0.1.5, 0.2.4; **L4:** 0.1.2, 0.1.5, 1.2.9, 4.1.6; **L5:** 0.1.2, 0.1.5, 2.1.7, 2.1.8, 4.6.5, 7.4.4, 7.7.3; **L6:** 0.1.2, 0.1.5, 0.2.4; **L7:** 0.1.2, 0.1.4, 0.1.5, 4.6.5, 4.8.1 | **L1:** SL.1.1, SL.K.6, L1.5a, L.1.5c, L.1.6; **L2:** SL.1.1, SL.1.3, L.1.1e, L.1.1g; **L3:** SL.K.3, SL.1.4, SL.K.6, L.1.1e, L.1.1g, L.1.1l, L.1.5c; **L4:** L.1.1l, L.1.5c, L.1.6; **L5:** RI/RL.1.1, W.1.7, W.1.8; **L6:** RI/RL.1.1, RI.1.2, RI.1.3, RI.1.4, RI.1.7, SL.K.2; **L7:** RI/RL.1.1, RI.1.2, RI.1.3, RI.1.7, SL.K.2 | ELPS 1–3, 5, 7–10 |
| **L1:** 0.1.2, 0.1.4, 0.1.5, 2.2.1; **L2:** 0.1.2, 0.1.4, 0.1.5, 2.2.1; **L3:** 0.1.2, 0.1.4, 0.1.5, 2.2.3; **L4:** 0.1.2, 0.1.4, 0.1.5, 2.2.1; **L5:** 0.1.2, 0.1.5, 1.9.1, 7.4.4, 7.7.3; **L6:** 0.1.2, 0.1.4, 0.1.5, 2.2.3; **L7:** 0.1.7, 2.2.1, 4.8.3 | **L1:** SL.1.1, L.1.1l, L.1.5c, L.1.6; **L2:** SL.1.1, L.1.1j, L.1.5c, L.1.6; **L3:** SL.K.2, SL.1.4, SL.K.6, L1.5a, L.1.5c, L.1.6; **L4:** RI.1.7, SL.K.3, SL.K.6; **L5:** W.1.7, W.1.8; **L6:** RI/RL.1.1, RI.1.2, RI.1.3, RI.1.4, RI.1.7, SL.K.2; **L7:** RI/RL.1.1, RI.1.2, RI.1.3, RI.1.7, SL.K.2 | ELPS 1–3, 5, 7–10 |
| **L1:** 0.1.2, 0.1.4, 0.1.5, 3.1.2, 3.6.1; **L2:** 0.1.2, 0.1.4, 0.1.5, 3.6.3, 3.6.4; **L3:** 0.1.2, 0.1.4, 0.1.5, 3.6.3; **L4:** 0.1.2, 0.1.4, 0.1.5, 1.9.7, 2.1.2, 2.2.1, 3.6.3; **L5:** 0.1.2, 0.1.5, 3.3.1, 3.3.2, 7.4.4, 7.7.3; **L6:** 0.1.2, 0.1.4, 0.1.5, 2.7.9, 3.1.2; **L7:** 0.1.2, 0.1.4, 0.1.5, 3.1.2. 3.6.3, 3.6.4 | **L1:** SL.1.1, L.1.5c, L.1.6; **L2:** SL.1.1, SL.K.6, L.1.5c; **L3:** L.1.1l, L.1.5c; **L4:** SL.1.4, SL.K.6; **L5:** RI/RL.1.1, RI.1.4, W.1.7, W.1.8; **L6:** RI/RL.1.1, RI.1.2, RI.1.3, RI.1.4, RI.1.7, SL.K.2, SL.K.3; **L7:** SL.K.3 | ELPS 1–3, 5, 7–10 |
| **L1:** 0.1.2, 0.1.4, 0.1.5, 4.1.8; **L2:** 0.1.2, 0.1.4, 0.1.5, 4.1.8; **L3:** 0.1.2, 0.1.4, 0.1.5, 4.1.6, 4.1.8; **L4:** 0.1.2, 0.1.4, 0.1.5, 4.1.2; **L5:** 0.1.2, 0.1.4, 0.1.5, 4.1.3, 7.4.4, 7.7.3; **L6:** 0.1.2, 0.1.5, 4.1.5, 4.1.7; **L7:** 0.1.2, 0.1.4, 0.1.5, 4.1.5, 4.1.7 | **L1:** SL.K.2, L.1.5a, L.1.5c, L.1.6; **L2:** SL.1.1, SL.K.2, SL.K.3, SL.1.4, SL.K.6, L.1.1k, L.1.5c, L.1.6; **L3:** SL.1.1, SL.K.6, L.1.5c, L.1.6; **L4:** SL.K.3, L.1.1k, L.1.1l; **L5:** RI/RL.1.1, W.1.7, W.1.8; **L6:** RI.1.2, RI.1.3, RI.1.4, RI.1.7 | ELPS 1–3, 5, 7–10 |

All units of *Future* meet most of the **EFF Content Standards**. For details, as well as for correlations to other state standards, go to www.pearsoneltusa.com/future 2e.

## SERIES CONSULTANT AND LEARNING EXPERT

**Sarah Lynn** is an ESOL teacher trainer, author, and curriculum design specialist. She has taught adult learners in the U.S. and abroad for decades, most recently at Harvard University's Center for Workforce Development. As a teacher-trainer and frequent conference presenter throughout the United States and Latin America, Ms. Lynn has led sessions and workshops on topics such as fostering student agency and resilience, brain-based teaching techniques, literacy and learning, and teaching in a multilevel classroom. Collaborating with program leaders, teachers, and students, she has developed numerous curricula for college and career readiness, reading and writing skill development, and contextualized content for adult English language learners. Ms. Lynn has co-authored several Pearson ELT publications, including *Business Across Cultures, Future, Future U.S. Citizens,* and *Project Success.* She holds a master's degree in TESOL from Teachers College, Columbia University.

## SERIES CONSULTANTS

**Ronna Magy** has worked as an ESOL classroom teacher, author, teacher-trainer, and curriculum development specialist. She served as the ESL Teacher Adviser in charge of professional development for the Division of Adult and Career Education of the Los Angeles Unified School District. She is a frequent conference presenter on the College and Career Readiness Standards (CCRS), the English Language Proficiency Standards (ELPS), and on the language, literacy, and soft skills needed for academic and workplace success. Ms. Magy has authored/ co-authored and trained teachers on modules for CALPRO, the California Adult Literacy Professional Development Project, including modules on integrating and contextualizing workforce skills in the ESOL classroom and evidence-based writing instruction. She is the author of adult ESL publications on English for the workplace, reading and writing, citizenship, and life skills and test preparation. Ms. Magy holds a master's degree in social welfare from the University of California at Berkeley.

**Federico Salas-Isnardi** has worked in adult education as a teacher, administrator, professional developer, materials writer, and consultant. He contributed to a number of state projects in Texas including the adoption of adult education content standards and the design of statewide professional development and accountability systems.

Over nearly 30 years he has conducted professional development seminars for thousands of teachers, law enforcement officers, social workers, and business people in the United States and abroad. His areas of concentration have been educational leadership, communicative competence, literacy, intercultural communication, citizenship, and diversity education. He has taught customized workplace ESOL and Spanish programs as well as high-school equivalence classes, citizenship and civics, labor market information seminars, and middle-school mathematics. Mr. Salas-Isnardi has been a contributing writer or series consultant for a number of ESL publications, and he has co-authored curriculum for site-based workforce ESL and Spanish classes.

Mr. Salas-Isnardi is a certified diversity trainer. He has a master's degree in Applied Linguistics and doctoral level coursework in adult education.

## AUTHOR

**Yvonne Wong Nishio** has been an adult school teacher, curriculum coordinator, counselor, and resource/demonstration teacher over the past 37 years in the Los Angeles Unified School District (LAUSD). She has taught all six ESL levels at Evans Community Adult School, one of the largest adult learning centers in the country. Ms. Nishio developed curriculum as well as materials for the Division of Adult and Career Education of LAUSD, including the *Asian Project,* which pioneered ESL materials culturally relevant to Asian Pacific immigrants; *Holidays in the U.S.,* which highlighted the multicultural roots of American holidays and customs; and *Places to See in the Los Angeles Area.* Ms. Nishio prepared a video program on domestic violence, *To Ensure Domestic Tranquility,* through a grant from the American Bar Association. Ms. Nishio's extensive work in ESL literacy includes contributions to the ESL Language Model Standards for Adult Education Programs established by the California Department of Education as well as the successful books *Longman ESL Literacy,* now in its third edition, and Longman *ESL Literacy Teacher's Resource Book.*

The Publisher would like to acknowledge the teachers, students, and survey and focus-group participants for their valuable input. Thank you to the following reviewers and consultants who made suggestions, contributed to this *Future* revision, and helped make *Future: English for Work, Life, and Academic Success* even better in this second edition. There are many more who also shared their comments and experiences using *Future*—a big thank you to all.

**Fuad Al-Daraweesh** The University of Toledo, Toledo, OH

**Denise Alexander** Bucks County Community College, Newtown, PA

**Isabel Alonso** Bergen Community College, Hackensack, NJ

**Veronica Avitia** LeBarron Park, El Paso, TX

**Maria Bazan-Myrick** Houston Community College, Houston, TX

**Sara M. Bulnes** Miami Dade College, Miami, FL

**Alexander Chakshiri** Santa Maria High School, Santa Maria, CA

**Scott C. Cohen,** M.A.Ed. Bergen Community College, Paramus, NJ

**Judit Criado Fiuza** Mercy Center, Bronx, NY

**Megan Ernst** Glendale Community College, Glendale, CA

**Rebecca Feit-Klein** Essex County College Adult Learning Center, West Caldwell, NJ

**Caitlin Floyd** Nationalities Service Center, Philadelphia, PA

**Becky Gould** International Community High School, Bronx, NY

**Ingrid Greenberg** San Diego Continuing Education, San Diego Community College District, San Diego, CA

**Steve Gwynne** San Diego Continuing Education, San Diego, CA

**Robin Hatfield,** M.Ed. Learning Institute of Texas, Houston, TX

**Coral Horton** Miami Dade College, Kendall Campus, Miami, FL

**Roxana Hurtado** Miami-Dade County Public Schools, Miami, FL

**Lisa Johnson** City College of San Francisco, San Francisco, CA

**Kristine R. Kelly** ATLAS @ Hamline University, St. Paul, MN

**Jennifer King** Austin Community College, Austin, TX

**Lia Lerner,** Ed.D. Burbank Adult School, Burbank, CA

**Ting Li** The University of Toledo, Ottawa Hills, OH

**Nichole M. Lucas** University of Dayton, Dayton, OH

**Ruth Luman** Modesto Junior College, Modesto, CA

**Josephine Majul** El Monte-Rosemead Adult School, El Monte, CA

**Dr. June Ohrnberger** Suffolk County Community College, Selden, NY

**Sue Park** The Learning Institute of Texas, Houston, TX

**Dr. Sergei Paromchik** Adult Education Department, Hillsborough County Public Schools, Tampa, FL

**Patricia Patton** Uniontown ESL, Uniontown, PA

**Matthew Piech** Amarillo College, Amarillo, TX

**Guillermo Rocha** Essex County College, NJ

**Audrene Rowe** Essex County School, Newark, NJ

**Naomi Sato** Glendale Community College, Glendale, CA

**Alejandra Solis** Lone Star College, Houston, TX

**Geneva Tesh** Houston Community College, Houston, TX

**Karyna Tytar** Lake Washington Institute of Technology, Kirkland, WA

**Miguel Veloso** Miami Springs Adult, Miami, FL

**Minah Woo** Howard Community College, Columbia, MD

# Unit

## 1 MEET YOUR TEACHER

Look at the teacher and student.
▶ Listen and point. Listen and repeat.

## 2 CLASSROOM INSTRUCTIONS

Ⓐ Look at the actions.
▶ Listen and point. Listen and repeat.

look

listen

point

repeat

read

write

open

close

Ⓑ **WORK TOGETHER.** Point to a picture in Exercise A. Say the action.

## 3 ASK FOR HELP

Look at the pictures. Complete the conversations.

~~Can you speak more slowly?~~     Can you repeat that?

What does this word mean?     What's this called in English?

**1.**

Where are you from?

I'm sorry. *Can you speak more slowly?*

Oh, sorry. Where are you from?

I'm from Korea.

**2.**

_____

It's a pencil sharpener.

Thank you.

**3.**

Can you help me?

Sure.

_____

Occupation? It means a job or career.

**4.**

Please turn to page 45.

I'm sorry. _____

Sure. Please turn to page 45.

## 4 SAY THE ALPHABET

Look at the alphabet.
▶ Listen and read. Listen and repeat.

Aa Bb Cc Dd Ee

Ff Gg Hh Ii Jj Kk

Ll Mm Nn Oo Pp

Qq Rr Ss Tt Uu

Vv Ww Xx Yy Zz

## 5 SAY NUMBERS

Look at the numbers.
▶ Listen and point. Listen and repeat.

| 1 2 3 4 5 6 7 8 9 10 |

## 6 LEARN ABOUT *FUTURE*

**A** Turn to page iii. Answer the questions.

**1.** How many units are in this book? _____     **2.** Which unit is about families? _____

**3.** Which unit is about health?     _____     **4.** Which unit is about food?     _____

**5.** Which unit is about shopping?   _____     **6.** Which unit is about school? _____

**B** Look in the back of your book. Find each section. Write the page numbers.

Map of the World                              _____

Word List                                     _____

Audio Script                                  _____

Index                                         _____

Map of the United States and Canada _____

**C** Look inside the front cover. How will you get the Pearson Practice English app with audio?

_____

# 1 Nice to Meet You

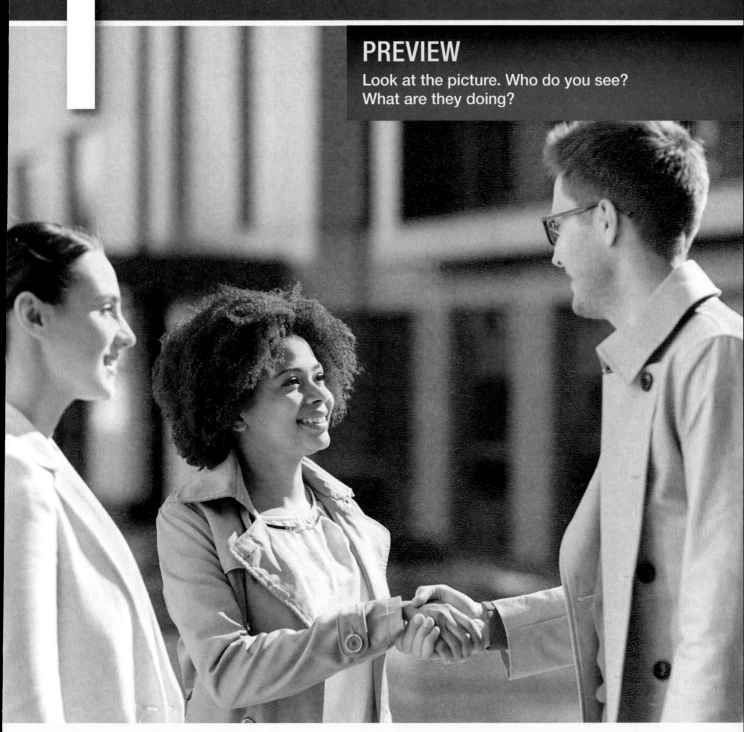

## PREVIEW

Look at the picture. Who do you see?
What are they doing?

## UNIT GOALS

- [ ] Introduce yourself
- [ ] Spell first and last names
- [ ] Say and write important numbers
- [ ] Talk about yourself
- [ ] Introduce someone

- [ ] Talk about people
- [ ] Read and write about greetings
- [ ] **Life skills:** Read and fill out a form
- [ ] **English at work:** Say hello

## Introduce Yourself

# Where are you from?

## 1 VOCABULARY: Countries

**A** Look at the map. What do you see?

▶ Listen and point. Listen and repeat.

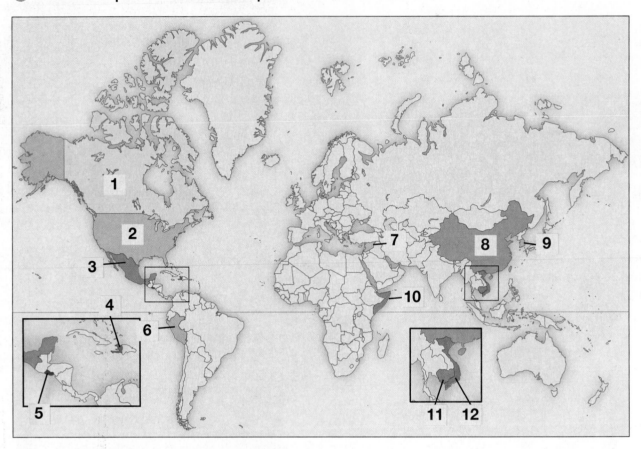

**B** ▶ Listen and read. Listen and repeat.

| | | |
|---|---|---|
| **1.** Canada | **2.** the United States | **3.** Mexico |
| **4.** Haiti | **5.** El Salvador | **6.** Peru |
| **7.** Syria | **8.** China | **9.** South Korea |
| **10.** Somalia | **11.** Cambodia | **12.** Vietnam |

**C** MAKE CONNECTIONS.  Point to your native country. Say the name.

## 2 CONVERSATION

**A** ▶ Listen. Listen and repeat.

**A:** Hello. My name is Rick Soto.
**B:** Hi. I'm May Chen.
**A:** Where are you from, May?
**B:** I'm from China.

**B** Practice the conversation.

**C** WORK TOGETHER. Make new conversations.

**A:** Hello. My name is _____.
**B:** Hi. I'm _____.
**A:** Where are you from, _____?
**B:** I'm from _____.

## Show what you know!

**1. TALK ABOUT IT.** Make new conversations. Talk to three classmates.

What's your name?
Where are you from?

**2. WRITE ABOUT IT.** Write the names and countries.

| | Name | Country |
|---|---|---|
| 1. | May | China |
| 2. | | |
| 3. | | |
| 4. | | |

I can introduce myself. ■                    I need more practice. ■

## Spell First and Last Names

# What's your name?

## 1 VOCABULARY: The alphabet

**A** ► Listen and point. Listen and repeat.

Aa Bb Cc Dd Ee
Ff Gg Hh Ii Jj Kk
Ll Mm Nn Oo Pp
Qq Rr Ss Tt Uu
Vv Ww Xx Yy Zz

**B** ► Listen. Write capital letters.

1. _____     2. _____     3. _____
4. _____     5. _____     6. _____
7. _____     8. _____     9. _____
10. _____    11. _____    12. _____

> B—capital letter
> b—lowercase letter

**C** WORK TOGETHER. Say a letter. Write the letter.

_____     _____     _____     _____     _____

**D** ► Listen. Write the words.

1. _____ _____ _____ _____     2. _____ _____
3. _____ _____ _____ _____     4. _____ _____ _____ _____ _____
5. _____ _____ _____          6. _____ _____ _____ _____

## 2 CONVERSATION

**A** ▶ **Listen. Listen and repeat.**

**A:** What's your name, please?
**B:** Ana Sol.
**A:** Spell your first name.
**B:** A-N-A.
**A:** Spell your last name.
**B:** S-O-L.

**B** Practice the conversation.

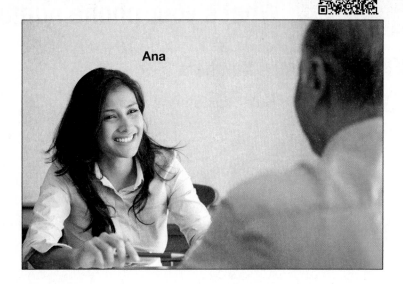

Ana

## Show what you know!

**1. TALK ABOUT IT.** Make new conversations. Talk to three classmates.

A: What's your name, please?
B: _____
A: Spell your first name.
B: _____
A: Spell your last name.
B: _____

**2. WRITE ABOUT IT.** Complete the chart.

| First Name | Last Name |
|---|---|
| 1. Ana | Sol |
| 2. | |
| 3. | |
| 4. | |

I can spell first and last names. ■                    I need more practice. ■

# Lesson 3 — What's your phone number?

## 1 VOCABULARY: Numbers 0–9

**A** ▶ Listen and point. Listen and repeat.

| 0 | 1 | 2 | 3 | 4 | 5 | 6 | 7 | 8 | 9 |
|---|---|---|---|---|---|---|---|---|---|
| zero | one | two | three | four | five | six | seven | eight | nine |

**B** ▶ Listen. Write the numbers.

a. _____  b. _____  c. _____  d. _____  e. _____  f. _____

**C** ▶ Listen. Circle the student ID.

**1.**

STUDENT ID
Name: John Pace
ID number: 02468

STUDENT ID
Name: John Potter
ID number: 01469

**2.**

STUDENT ID
Name: Sue Gao
ID number: 78396

STUDENT ID
Name: Grace Tang
ID number: 65378

**3.**

STUDENT ID
Name: Anne Joseph
ID number: 05376

STUDENT ID
Name: Ann Crane
ID number: 06735

# Talk About People

## 3 GRAMMAR: *You are, we are, they are*

| | | |
|---|---|---|
| You and Su **are** from China. | Tim and I **are** from Peru. | Joan and Kim **are** students. |
| **You are** from China. | **We are** from Peru. | **They are** students. |
| **You're** from China. | **We're** from Peru. | **They're** students. |

**Write three sentences. Use *you, we, they* and *you're, we're, they're*.**

> you are = you're
> we are = we're
> they are = they're

**1.** Carlo and Ana / from Brazil

*Carlo and Ana are from Brazil.*

*They are from Brazil.*

_____

**2.** Mr. Edison and you / good teachers

_____

_____

_____

**3.** Edna and I / from Haiti

_____

_____

_____

## Show what you know!

**1. WRITE ABOUT IT.** Write two sentences about your classmates.

_____ *and* _____ *are* _____.

*They are* _____.

**2. TELL THE CLASS.** Read your sentences.

*Dan and Ana are students. They are from Haiti.*

I can talk about people. ■          I need more practice. ■

# Joe is a student.

## 1 READING

**A** ► Listen and read.

### Adult Education Center

| **First Name** | **Middle Name** | **Last Name** |
|---|---|---|
| Joe | Lee | Baker |

| **Phone Number** | **Place of Birth** |
|---|---|
| 760-555-7765 | Canada |

**Student ID Number**
78031

**B** Read the form again. Circle *Yes* or *No*.

| | | |
|---|---|---|
| **1.** This is Joe's form. | Yes | No |
| **2.** His middle name is Baker. | Yes | No |
| **3.** His last name is Lee. | Yes | No |
| **4.** Joe is a student. | Yes | No |
| **5.** He is from China. | Yes | No |
| **6.** His phone number is 7765. | Yes | No |
| **7.** Joe's student ID number is 78031. | Yes | No |

**C** **WORK TOGETHER.** Compare your answers.

## 2 WRITING

**A** Complete the sentences.

1. My first name is _____.
2. My last name is _____.
3. My phone number is _____.
4. I'm from _____.
5. My student ID number is _____.

**B** Fill out the form. Use your information in Exercise A.

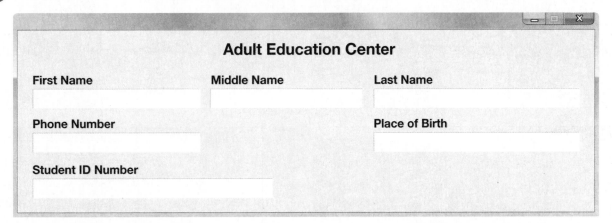

**Adult Education Center**

First Name

Middle Name

Last Name

Phone Number

Place of Birth

Student ID Number

**C** **WORK TOGETHER.** Read your classmate's form. Is the form complete?

**D** GO ONLINE.

1. Find your school's website.
2. Write the school's phone number.

_____

I can read and fill out a form. ▪                    I need more practice. ▪

# 8

## This is Ivan.

### 1 LISTENING

**A** Look at each picture. What do you see?

**B** ► Listen to the story.

# Read and Write About Greetings

## 2 READING

**A** ► Read and listen.

This is Ivan. He is a student.
He says hello to his classmates and smiles.
In his school, some students say hello and shake hands.
Some students say hello and hug.
Some students say hello and bow.
Other students say hello and kiss.

**B** Circle *Yes* or *No*.

1. Ivan says hello.        Yes     No
2. Ivan smiles.            Yes     No
3. Ivan hugs.              Yes     No
4. Some students bow.      Yes     No
5. Ivan shakes hands.      Yes     No

## 3 WRITING

**A** MAKE CONNECTIONS. Talk about people in your native country.

1. Do they say hello and smile?
2. Do they shake hands?
3. Do they hug?
4. Do they bow?
5. Do they kiss?

**B** Complete the sentences.

1. In my native country, some people say hello and _____.
2. Other people say hello and _____.
3. In my school, some students say hello and _____.
4. Other students say hello and _____.

**C** WORK TOGETHER. Read your sentences.

I can read and write about greetings. ■          I need more practice. ■

# Lesson 9 Sam is at work.

Sam          Customer

## 1 READING

Sam is a greeter.
He works in a store.
He says hello to customers.

## 2 CONVERSATION AT WORK

**A** Complete the conversation. Write the correct words.

**Sam:** _____ to Buy Best.

| Welcome | Hello |
|---------|-------|

**Customer:** _____.

| Thank you | You're welcome |
|-----------|----------------|

**Sam:** Can I help you?

**Customer:** No _____. I'm fine.

| hello | thank you |
|-------|-----------|

**B** Practice the conversation.

**C** Role-play the conversation with new information.

I can say hello. ■                          I need more practice. ■

# VOCABULARY REVIEW

**A** ▶ **LISTEN.** Listen and repeat.

| | | | |
|---|---|---|---|
| Cambodia | eight | first name | five |
| hug | kiss | last name | nine |
| phone number | place of birth | shake hands | smile |
| Somalia | three | the United States | Vietnam |

**B** Complete the chart. Use the words in Exercise A.

| Countries | Ways to Say Hello | Numbers | Words on a Form |
|---|---|---|---|
| | | | |
| | | | |
| | | | |
| | | | |

**C** Write *he*, *she*, or *they*.

1. _____

2. _____

3. _____

# GRAMMAR REVIEW

**A** Complete the sentences. Write *am*, *is,* or *are*.

1. We _____*are*_____ teachers.
2. He _____ from China.
3. They _____ from Vietnam.
4. She _____ a teacher.
5. I _____ Lily.
6. You _____ from Canada.
7. I _____ a teacher.
8. You _____ students.
9. She _____ from Peru.
10. We _____ from Mexico.
11. He _____ a student.

**B** Rewrite the sentences from Exercise A. Use contractions.

1. _We're teachers._____
2. _____
3. _____
4. _____
5. _____
6. _____
7. _____
8. _____
9. _____
10. _____
11. _____

## ROLE-PLAY.

**A** Introduce yourself.

**A:** Hello. I'm _____. What's your name?

**B:** Hi. I'm _____. Nice to meet you.

**A:** Nice to meet you, too.

**B:** Where are you from?

**A:** I'm from _____. Where are you from?

**B:** I'm from _____.

**B** Walk around the room. Practice the conversation with more classmates.

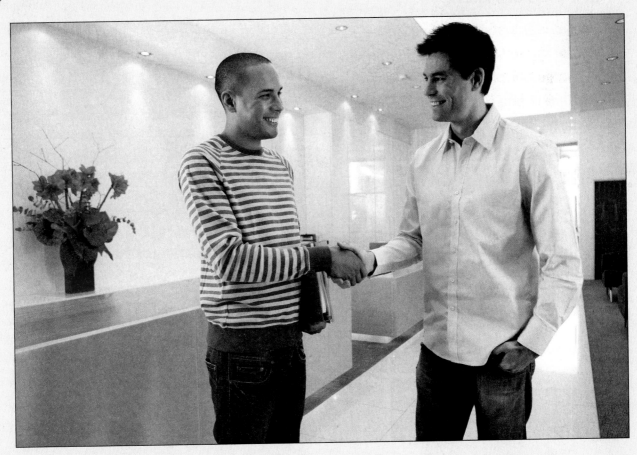

# LIFE SKILLS AND WRITING REVIEW

## 1 LIFE SKILLS: Read a form

### ABC English Center
#### Student Information Form

| First Name | Middle Name | Last Name |
|---|---|---|
| Marta | | Cruz |

| Phone Number | Place of Birth |
|---|---|
| 202-555-1234 | El Salvador |

**Student ID Number**
63588

Answer the questions.

1. What is the student's first name? _____
2. What is the student's last name? _____
3. What is her phone number? _____
4. Where is she from? _____
5. What is her student ID number? _____

## 2 WRITE ABOUT YOURSELF

Fill out the form. Use your information.

### ABC English Center
#### Student Information Form

| First Name | Middle Name | Last Name |
|---|---|---|
| | | |

| Phone Number | Place of Birth |
|---|---|
| | |

**Student ID Number**

**Unit Review:** Go back to page 5. Which unit goals can you check off?

## PREVIEW

Look at the picture. Who do you see?
What are they doing?

# UNIT GOALS

☐ Ask for things in class
☐ Follow classroom instructions
☐ Talk about places in a school
☐ Describe locations
☐ Talk about study skills

☐ Read and write about classrooms
☐ **Life skills:** Understand a form
☐ **English at work:** Help someone fill
out a form

# Ask for Things in Class

## Do you have a pen?

## 1 VOCABULARY: Classroom items

**A** Look at the pictures. What do you see?

**1**

**2**

**3**

**4**

**5**

**6**

**7**

**8**

**9**

**B** ▶ Listen and read. Listen and repeat.

**1.** a dictionary app

**2.** a pen

**3.** a book

**4.** an eraser

**5.** a piece of paper

**6.** a phone

**7.** a notebook

**8.** a pencil

**9.** a backpack

**C** MAKE CONNECTIONS. Look around the classroom. What do you see?

## 2 CONVERSATION

**A** ▶ **Listen. Listen and repeat.**

**A:** Excuse me. Do you have a pencil?
**B:** No, I don't.
**A:** Do you have a pen?
**B:** Yes, I do. Here you go.
**A:** Thanks.

**B** **Practice the conversation.**

**C** **WORK TOGETHER.** Make new conversations.

**A:** Excuse me. Do you have _____?
**B:** No, I don't.
**A:** Do you have _____?
**B:** Yes, I do. Here you go.
**A:** Thanks.

### Show what you know!

**1. WRITE ABOUT IT.** What do you have? Write classroom objects.

_____ *a book* _____        _____

_____        _____

_____        _____

**2. TELL THE CLASS.** What do you have? Tell your classmates.

*I have a book and a pen.*

I can ask for things in class. ◻            I need more practice. ◻

# Lesson 2 — Please close your books.

## 1 VOCABULARY: Classroom instructions

**A** Look at the pictures. What do you see?

**B** Watch and listen to your teacher.

**C** ▶ Listen and read. Listen and repeat.

| | | |
|---|---|---|
| **1.** Turn on the light. | **2.** Take out your pencil. | **3.** Open your book. |
| **4.** Close your book. | **5.** Put away your book. | **6.** Turn off the light. |

**D** **WORK TOGETHER.** Student A: Say a classroom instruction. Student B: Point to the picture. Take turns.

# Follow Classroom Instructions

## 2 CONVERSATION

**A** ▶ Listen. Listen and repeat.

**A:** It is time for a test. Please close your books.
**B:** OK.
**A:** Use a pencil. Don't use a pen.

**B** Practice the conversation.

## 3 GRAMMAR: Imperatives

| | |
|---|---|
| **Use** a pencil. | **Don't use** a pencil.<br>**Do not use** a pencil. |
| **Put away** your books. | **Don't put away** your books.<br>**Do not put away** your books. |

do not = don't

**A** Write sentences with *don't*.

1. Open your backpack.  <u>*Don't open your backpack.*</u>
2. Use a dictionary app.  _____
3. Put away your notebook.  _____
4. Turn off your phone.  _____
5. Take out your book.  _____
6. Close the door.  _____

**B** ▶ Listen and check your answers. Listen and repeat.

### Show what you know!

1. **TALK ABOUT IT.** Student A: Give an instruction. Student B: Do the action.

2. **WRITE ABOUT IT.** Write the instructions.

   *Close your book.*

I can follow classroom instructions. ■          I need more practice. ☐

# Where is the teacher?

## 1 VOCABULARY: Places in a school

**A** ▶ Listen and point. Listen and repeat.

**B** ▶ Listen and read. Listen and repeat.

1. library
2. office
3. testing room
4. cafeteria
5. restroom
6. classroom
7. bookstore
8. computer lab

**C** Write the places in your school.

_____office_____   _____   _____

_____   _____   _____

**D** WORK TOGETHER. Show your partner your words. Add more words.

## 2 CONVERSATION

**A** ▶ Listen. Listen and repeat.

**A:** Where is the teacher?
**B:** He's in the library.

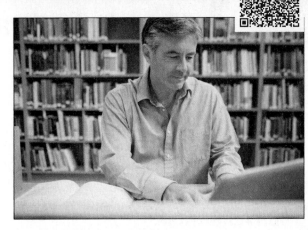

**B** Practice the conversation.

**C** Complete the conversations.

**1.**

**A:** Where is the teacher?
**B:** He's in the _____.

**2.**

**A:** Where is Sara?
**B:** She's in the _____.

**3.**

**A:** Where is your book?
**B:** It's in the _____.

**4.**

**A:** Where is your backpack?
**B:** It's in the _____.

**D** ▶ Listen and check your answers. Listen and repeat.

### Show what you know!

**1. WRITE ABOUT IT.** Make a new conversation.

A: Where is _____?
B: _____ is in the _____. Where is _____?
A: _____ is in the _____.

**2. TALK ABOUT IT.** Practice your conversation.

I can talk about places in a school. ☐          I need more practice. ☐

# Where is the library?

## 1 VOCABULARY: *Next to*

▶ Listen and point. Listen and repeat.

The bookstore is **next to** the testing room.
The testing room is **next to** the bookstore.

bookstore

testing room

## 2 CONVERSATION

**A** ▶ Listen. Listen and repeat.

**A:** Excuse me. Where is the bookstore?
**B:** It's next to the testing room.
**A:** Thanks.

**B** Practice the conversation.

**C** **WORK TOGETHER.** Look at the pictures. Make new conversations. Use *next to*.

**Conversation 1**

classroom

bookstore

office

**Conversation 2**

restroom

computer lab

library

**A:** Excuse me. Where is the _____?
**B:** It's next to the _____.
**A:** Thanks.

## 3 VOCABULARY: *Across from*

▶ Listen and point. Listen and repeat.

The library is **across from** the office.
The office is **across from** the library.

## 4 CONVERSATION

**A** ▶ Listen. Listen and repeat.

**A:** Excuse me. Where is the library?
**B:** It's across from the office.
**A:** Thanks.

**B** Practice the conversation.

**C** **WORK TOGETHER.**
Look at the picture.
Make new conversations.
Use *across from*.

**A:** Excuse me. Where is the
_____?
**B:** It's across from the
_____.
**A:** Thanks.

## Show what you know!

**1. WRITE ABOUT IT.** Write about places in your school.

The _____ is next to the _____.
The _____ is across from the _____.

**2. TALK ABOUT IT.** Talk about the places.

The library is next to the office.

I can describe locations. ■                    I need more practice. ■

# What's your first name?

## 1 VOCABULARY

**A** ▶ Listen and repeat.

Mr.          Mrs.          Ms.

married

Miss          Ms.          Mr.

single

male

female

**B** ▶ Listen. Circle *M* (male) or *F* (female). Then listen and repeat.

1.   M   F            2.   M   F
3.   M   F            4.   M   F

## 2 READING

**A** ▶ Listen and read.

● ● ●

### Vista Learning Center

○ Mr.      **Last Name**        **First Name**
◉ Mrs.     Lopez               Alexa
○ Miss     **Place of Birth**
○ Ms.      Mexico              ◉ Female  ○ Male

**Class**               **Teacher**
English 100            Mr. Chen

**B** Read the form again. Circle *Yes* or *No*.

| | | |
|---|---|---|
| **1.** Alexa is married. | Yes | No |
| **2.** Alexa is from England. | Yes | No |
| **3.** Alexa is male. | Yes | No |
| **4.** Alexa is in English 100. | Yes | No |
| **5.** Alexa's teacher is Mr. Lopez. | Yes | No |

# Life Skills: Understand a Form

## 3 WRITING

**A** Answer the questions.

1. What is your first name? _____
2. What is your last name? _____
3. What class are you in? _____
4. What is your teacher's name? _____
5. Where are you from? _____

**B** Fill out the form. Use your information in Exercise A.

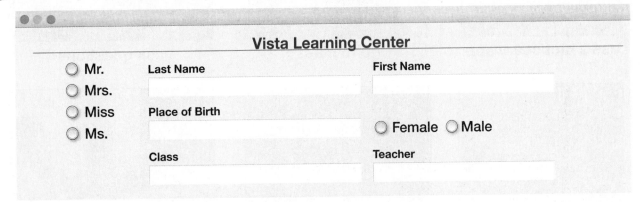

**C** WORK TOGETHER. Read your classmate's form. Is the form complete?

**D** GO ONLINE.

1. Find a form online.
2. Fill out the form with your information.

I can understand a form. ■                    I need more practice. ■

# How do you study English?

## 1 VOCABULARY: Study skills

▶ Listen and point. Listen and repeat.

**use a dictionary app**

**go to class**

**ask questions**

**read signs**

**write new words**

**practice with my classmates**

## 2 CONVERSATION

**A** ▶ Listen. Listen and repeat.

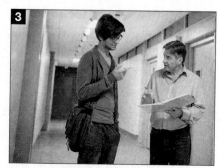

**A:** How do you study English?
**B:** I practice with my classmates, and I write new words.
**A:** That's great!

**B** Practice the conversation.

**C** WORK TOGETHER. Make new conversations.

**A:** How do you study English?
**B:** I _____, and I _____.

# Talk About Study Skills

## 3 GRAMMAR: Simple present: *I, you, we, they*

| | |
|---|---|
| **I practice** with my classmates. | **We write** new words. |
| **You use** a dictionary app. | **They ask** questions. |

**A** Complete the paragraph. Use words from the box.

Rosa

| go | practice | read | ~~study~~ | use | write |
|---|---|---|---|---|---|

My name is Rosa. I _____*study*_____ English. I _____
to class every day. I _____ English with my
classmates. We _____ new words in our notebooks. I _____
a dictionary app on my phone. On the street, I _____ signs. How do you
study English?

**B** Complete the sentences. Use words from the box.

| go | practice | read | write |
|---|---|---|---|

**1.** I _____ to class every day.

**2.** They _____ signs on the street.

**3.** We _____ with our classmates.

**4.** You _____ new words.

## Show what you know!

**1. TALK ABOUT IT.** Ask your classmates: *How do you study English?*
Check (✓) the boxes.

- ☐ go to class
- ☐ ask questions
- ☐ practice with my classmates
- ☐ write new words
- ☐ use a dictionary app
- ☐ read signs

**2. WRITE ABOUT IT.** Write sentences.

We ask questions. We read signs.

| I can talk about study skills. ■ | I need more practice. ■ |
|---|---|

# Read and Write About Classrooms

## This is Lan.

### 1 | LISTENING

**A** Look at each picture. What do you see?

**B** ▶ Listen to the story.

# Read and Write About Classrooms

## 2 READING

**A** ▶ Read and listen.

> This is Lan.
> In her native country, students do not talk in class.
> They listen to the teacher.
> In the United States, students talk in groups.
> Students ask questions.
> The teacher listens to the students.

**B** Circle *Yes* or *No*.

| | | | |
|---|---|---|---|
| **1.** Lan is from the United States. | Yes | No |
| **2.** In Lan's native country, students talk in class. | Yes | No |
| **3.** In the United States, students ask questions. | Yes | No |
| **4.** In the United States, the teacher listens to the students. | Yes | No |

## 3 WRITING

**A** MAKE CONNECTIONS. Talk about students in your native country.

**1.** Do students talk in class?

**2.** Do students ask questions in class?

**B** Complete the sentences.

**1.** In my native country, students _____ in class.

**2.** They _____ in class.

**3.** In the United States, students _____ in class.

**4.** They _____ in class.

**C** WORK TOGETHER. Read your sentences.

I can read and write about classrooms. ■    I need more practice. ■

# English at Work: Help Someone Fill Out a Form

## Alma is at work.

Alma

Student

## 1 READING

Alma is a secretary.
She works in a school.
She helps a student fill out a form.

## 2 CONVERSATION AT WORK

**A** Complete the conversation. Write the correct words.

**Alma:** What is your _____?

**Student:** My last _____ is Sanchez.

**Alma:** OK. What is your _____ name?

**Student:** My _____ is Rosa.
My name is Rosa Sanchez.

**Alma:** Great! Write your first and last name on the form here.

| | |
|---|---|
| classroom | last name |
| name | teacher |
| first | school |
| teacher's name | first name |

**B** Practice the conversation.

**C** Role-play the conversation with your information.

I can help someone fill out a form. ▪        I need more practice. ▪

# VOCABULARY REVIEW

**A** ▶ **LISTEN.** Listen and repeat.

| | | | | |
|---|---|---|---|---|
| book | cafeteria | close | computer lab | library |
| notebook | office | open | pen | pencil |
| put away | restroom | take out | turn on | |

**B** Write the words.

**C** Complete the chart. Use the words in Exercise A.

| Classroom Items | Places in a School | Classroom Instructions |
|---|---|---|
| | | |
| | | |
| | | |
| | | |
| | | |

# GRAMMAR REVIEW

**A** Write sentences.

1. _Open your book._      Don't open your book.
2. Use a dictionary app.      _____
3. Turn on your phone.      _____
4. _____      Don't open the door.
5. Turn off the light.      _____
6. _____      Don't put away your notebook.

**B** Complete the sentences. Use words from the box.

| ask | eat | go | ~~study~~ | talk | use | write |
|-----|-----|-----|--------|------|-----|-------|

1. I _____study_____ English.
2. We _____ in groups.
3. We _____ to school every day.
4. They _____ in the cafeteria.
5. I _____ a dictionary app on my phone.
6. They _____ in their notebooks.
7. I _____ questions in the classroom.

**C** How do you study? Write sentences. Use words from the box.

| | |
|---|---|
| ask questions | read signs |
| ~~go to class~~ | use a dictionary app |
| practice with my friends | write new words |

_I go to class._ _____

_____

_____

_____

_____

_____

## ROLE-PLAY.

**Student A**
Ask about places in the school.

**Student B**
Help Student A. Look at the map.
Use *across from* or *next to*.

**A:** Excuse me. Where is the _____?
**B:** It's next to the _____.
**A:** Thanks.

**Switch roles.**
**B:** Excuse me. Where is the _____?
**A:** It's across from the _____.
**B:** Thanks.

## 1 LIFE SKILLS: Understand a form

**Student Information Form**
**Mountain View School**

○ Mr.
● Mrs.
○ Miss
○ Ms.

**Last Name**
Antar

**First Name**
Haya

**Class**
English 101

**Teacher**
Mr. Jacobs

**Place of Birth**
Syria

Read the form. Circle *Yes* or *No*.

| | | |
|---|---|---|
| 1. The student's first name is Antar. | Yes | No |
| 2. The student is married. | Yes | No |
| 3. The student is in English 101. | Yes | No |
| 4. The student's teacher is Mr. Antar. | Yes | No |
| 5. The student is from Syria. | Yes | No |

## 2 WRITE ABOUT YOURSELF

Fill out of the form. Use your information.

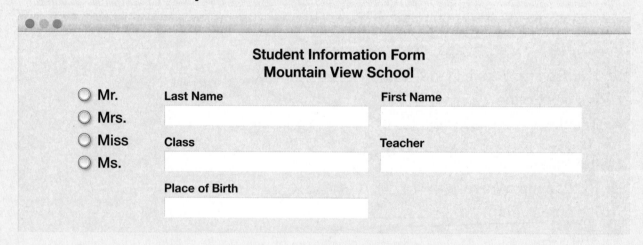

**Student Information Form**
**Mountain View School**

○ Mr.
○ Mrs.
○ Miss
○ Ms.

**Last Name**

**First Name**

**Class**

**Teacher**

**Place of Birth**

**Unit Review:** Go back to page 27. Which unit goals can you check off?

# 3

## PREVIEW

Look at the picture. Who do you see?
What is he doing?

## UNIT GOALS

- ☐ Say the time
- ☐ Talk about schedules
- ☐ Talk about daily activities
- ☐ Talk about your weekly schedule
- ☐ Read and write about time

- ☐ **Life skills:** Read and write a weekly schedule
- ☐ **English at work:** Talk about schedules

# What time is it?

## 1 VOCABULARY: Numbers and time

**A** Look at the numbers.

▶ Listen and point. Listen and repeat.

| 0 | 1 | 2 | 3 | 4 | 5 | 6 | 7 | 8 | 9 |
|---|---|---|---|---|---|---|---|---|---|
| 10 | 11 | 12 | 13 | 14 | 15 | 16 | 17 | 18 | 19 |

| 20 | 21 | 22 | 23 | 24 | 25 | 26 | 27 | 28 | 29 |
|----|----|----|----|----|----|----|----|----|----|
| 30 | 31 | 32 | 33 | 34 | 35 | 36 | 37 | 38 | 39 |

| 40 | 41 | 42 | 43 | 44 | 45 | 46 | 47 | 48 | 49 |
|----|----|----|----|----|----|----|----|----|----|
| 50 | 51 | 52 | 53 | 54 | 55 | 56 | 57 | 58 | 59 |

**B** **WORK TOGETHER.** Point to a number. Say the number.

**C** ▶ Listen. Circle the number.

a. 10    20      b. 17    19
c. 24    14      d. 30    13
e. 15    50      f. 42    14
g. 26    36      h. 27    47

**D** ▶ Listen and point. Listen and repeat.

1. 1:00
2. 1:05
3. 1:15
4. 1:20
5. 1:30
6. 1:40
7. 1:45
8. 1:50

## 2 CONVERSATION

**A** ▶ Listen. Listen and repeat.

**A:** What time is it?

**B:** It's 1:00.

**B** Practice the conversation.

**C** Write the times.

1. _____ 2. _____ 3. _____ 4. _____

5. _____ 6. _____ 7. _____ 8. _____

**D** **WORK TOGETHER.** Point to the times. Make new conversations.

### Show what you know!

**TALK ABOUT IT.** What time is it? Ask and answer. Take turns.

A: What time is it?

B: It's 8:05.

| I can say the time. ■ | I need more practice. ■ |

# What time is your break?

## 1 VOCABULARY: Talking about times

▶ Listen and point. Listen and repeat.

Class **is at** 9:00.

Class **is over at** 12:30.

My break is **from** 10:45 **to** 11:15.

## 2 CONVERSATION

**A** ▶ Listen. Listen and repeat.

**A:** What time is your English class?
**B:** It's from 9:00 to 12:30.
**A:** What time is your break?
**B:** It's from 10:45 to 11:15.

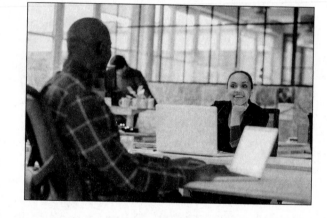

**B** Circle *Yes* or *No*.

| | | |
|---|---|---|
| **1.** The class is at 9:00. | Yes | No |
| **2.** The class is over at 12:00. | Yes | No |
| **3.** The break is at 10:45. | Yes | No |

**C** Practice the conversation.

**D** WORK TOGETHER. Make new conversations.

**A:** What time is your English class?
**B:** It's from _____ to _____.
**A:** What time is your break?
**B:** It's from _____ to _____.

## 3 GRAMMAR: *From / to, at*

| | |
|---|---|
| My class is **from** 9:00 **to** 12:30. | My class is **at** 9:00.<br>My class is over **at** 12:30. |
| My break is **from** 10:45 **to** 11:15. | My break is **at** 10:45.<br>My break is over **at** 11:15. |

**A** Complete the sentences. Use *from, to,* or *at.*

1. My English class is _____*at*_____ 1:00.
2. Lunch is _____ 12:00 _____ 1:00.
3. Our class is _____ 4:30.
4. His work day is over _____ 5:00.
5. Ella's break is _____ 3:15 _____ 3:30.

**B** Write sentences. Use *from, to,* or *at.*

1. Lunch is / 11:00 / 11:45   _Lunch is from 11:00 to 11:45._
2. English class is / 6:30   _____
3. The break is / 8:00 / 8:15   _____
4. Our class is over / 9:30   _____
5. Her class is / 2:00 / 3:30   _____

## Show what you know!

**1. WRITE ABOUT IT.** What is your class or work schedule?

My _____ is from _____ to _____.
My break is at _____. It is over at _____.

**2. TELL THE CLASS.** Talk about your class or work schedule.

My English class is from 9:00 to 11:30.
My break is at 10:30. It is over at 10:45.

# What time do you go to work?

## 1 VOCABULARY: Daily activities

**A** Look at the pictures. What do you see?

▶ Listen and point. Listen and repeat.

**B** ▶ Listen and read. Listen and repeat.

| | | |
|---|---|---|
| **1.** get up | **2.** take a shower | **3.** get dressed |
| **4.** eat breakfast | **5.** go to work | **6.** eat lunch |
| **7.** go to school | **8.** get home | **9.** go to sleep |

**C** Answer the questions.

1. What time do you get up?      _I get up at 6:30._
2. What time do you eat lunch?   _____
3. What time do you get home?    _____
4. What time do you go to sleep? _____

# Talk About Daily Activities

## 2 CONVERSATION

**A** ▶ Listen. Listen and repeat.

A: What time do you go to work?
B: I go to work at 6:00. What time do you go to work?
A: I go to work at 10:00.

**B** Practice the conversation.

**C** WORK TOGETHER. Make new conversations.

A: What time do you _____?
B: I _____ at _____.
    What time do you _____?
A: I _____ at _____.

---

### Show what you know!

**1. WRITE ABOUT IT.** What time do you do things? Write times.

I get up _____.
I eat breakfast _____.
I go to work _____.
I go to school _____.
I get home _____.
I go to sleep _____.

**2. TALK ABOUT IT.** Ask and answer questions.

A: What time do you get up?
B: I get up at 6:00.

---

I can talk about daily activities. ☐          I need more practice. ☐

# When do you work?

## 1 VOCABULARY: Days of the week

▶ Listen and point. Listen and repeat.

| Sunday | Monday | Tuesday | Wednesday | Thursday | Friday | Saturday |
|---|---|---|---|---|---|---|
| go to library | work | work | work | work | work | school |

Start days of the week with a capital letter.

## 2 CONVERSATION

**A** ▶ Listen. Listen and repeat.

**A:** When do you work, Nora?
**B:** I work from Monday to Friday.
**A:** When do you go to school?
**B:** I go to school on Saturday.
**A:** You're really busy!

Nora

**B** Practice the conversation.

**C** ▶ Listen and read.

Hi, I'm Nora. I'm very busy. I work from Monday to Friday. I go to school on Saturday. I go to the library on Sunday.

**D** Circle *Yes* or *No*.

1. Nora works from Monday to Friday.    Yes    No
2. She goes to school on Sunday.    Yes    No
3. She works on Wednesday.    Yes    No
4. She goes to the library on Saturday.    Yes    No

# Talk About Your Weekly Schedule

## 3 GRAMMAR: *From / to, on*

| | |
|---|---|
| I work **from** Monday **to** Friday. | I go to school **on** Monday and Wednesday. |

**A** Complete the sentences. Use *from, to,* or *on*.

1. I work _____*from*_____ Monday _____*to*_____ Thursday.
2. We play soccer _____ Tuesday.
3. I go to school _____ Friday.
4. They go to school _____ Wednesday _____ Friday.
5. I eat lunch at home _____ Sunday.

**B** ▶ Listen and check your answers. Listen and repeat.

## Show what you know!

### 1. WRITE ABOUT IT. Write your weekly schedule.

| | Sunday | Monday | Tuesday | Wednesday | Thursday | Friday | Saturday |
|---|---|---|---|---|---|---|---|
| work | | | | | | | |
| school | | | | | | | |

### 2. TALK ABOUT IT. Talk about your weekly schedule.

*I work from Tuesday to Saturday. I go to school on Monday.*

| | |
|---|---|
| I can talk about my weekly schedule. ■ | I need more practice. ■ |

# Felipe works on Monday and Tuesday.

## 1 READING

**A** Read Felipe's weekly schedule.

| | |
|---|---|
| SUN | 10:30–1:00 study |
| | 1:00–10:00 rest! |
| MON | 9:00–5:00 work |
| | 12:00–12:45 break |
| TUE | 8:30–2:00 school |
| WED | 9:00–5:00 work |
| | 12:00–12:45 break |
| THU | 10:30–3:00 school |
| | 6:00–7:30 English class |
| FRI | 9:30–2:30 work |
| | 12:00–12:45 break |
| SAT | 11:00–2:00 practice English |

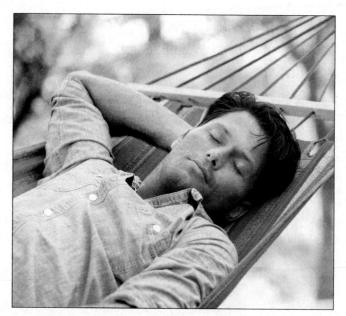

Felipe is **resting**.

**B** Complete the sentences.

1. Felipe works from _____ to _____ on Monday.
2. His break is from _____ to _____ on Monday, Wednesday, and _____.
3. Felipe goes to school from _____ to _____ on Tuesday.
4. He goes to school from 10:30 to 3:00 on _____.
5. He works from _____ to _____ on Friday.
6. He practices English from _____ to _____ on _____.
7. His English class is from _____ to _____ on _____.
8. Felipe rests from _____ to _____ on _____.

# Life Skills: Read and Write a Weekly Schedule

## 2 WRITING

**A** Complete your weekly schedule.

**B** Answer the questions.

1. When do you work?

2. When do you go to school?

3. When do you practice English?

4. When do you study?

**C** GO ONLINE.

1. Find the class schedule for your school online.
2. Write sentences.

   *English class is on Monday and Wednesday.*

I can read and write a weekly schedule. ■      I need more practice. ■

**Read and Write About Time**

# Manny gets up at 6:00.

## 1 LISTENING

**A** Look at each picture. What do you see?

**B** ▶ Listen to the story.

# Read and Write About Time

## 2 READING

**A** ▶ Read and listen.

> Manny gets up at 6:00.
> He gets to work at 7:55. He starts work at 8:00. He is on time.
> He goes to school after work.
> He gets to class at 5:45. Class starts at 6:00. He is early.
> Manny meets friends on Saturday. But he is late!

**B** Circle *Yes* or *No*.

| | | |
|---|---|---|
| **1.** Manny starts work at 7:00. | Yes | No |
| **2.** He is late for work. | Yes | No |
| **3.** Class starts at 6:45. | Yes | No |
| **4.** Manny is early for class. | Yes | No |
| **5.** He is late on Saturday. | Yes | No |

## 3 WRITING

**A** **MAKE CONNECTIONS.** Talk about people in your native country.

1. Do people go to work on time?
2. Do people go to school on time?
3. Do people meet friends on time?

**B** Complete the sentences.

1. In my native country, people go to work _____.
2. They go to school _____.
3. They meet friends _____.

**C** **WORK TOGETHER.** Read your sentences.

| | |
|---|---|
| I can read and write about time. ■ | I need more practice. ■ |

# Wei is at work.

## 1 READING

Wei is a manager.
He works in a supermarket.
He talks about his employee's schedule.

## 2 CONVERSATION AT WORK

**A** Complete the conversation. Write the correct words.

| | |
|---|---|
| **Wei:** | It is 9:10. You're _____. |
| **Employee:** | _____! |
| **Wei:** | Work _____ at 9:00.<br>Why are you late? |
| **Employee:** | The bus was _____.<br>I'm sorry. |
| **Wei:** | OK. Please call me next time. |

| late | early |
|---|---|
| I'm sorry | Thank you |
| starts | stops |
| on time | late |

**B** Practice the conversation.

**C** Role-play the conversation with new information.

I can talk about schedules. ■    I need more practice. ■

# VOCABULARY REVIEW

**A** ▶ **LISTEN. Write the numbers.**

1. _____    2. _____    3. _____    4. _____    5. _____

6. _____    7. _____    8. _____    9. _____    10. _____

**B** Look at the numbers in Exercise A. Write them in the correct order.

____   ____   ____   ____   ____   ____   ____   ____   ____   ____

**C** Write the days of the week in the correct order.

| Friday | Monday | Saturday | Sunday | Thursday | Tuesday | Wednesday |

1. _____    2. _____    3. _____

4. _____    5. _____    6. _____

7. _____

**D** Write the daily activities.

| eat breakfast | get home | go to school | go to sleep | go to work | take a shower |

1. _____    2. _____    3. _____

4. _____    5. _____    6. _____

**A** Complete the sentences. Use *from, to, at,* or *on.*

1. Class is _____ *at* _____ 8:00.

2. I work _____ Monday _____ Thursday.

3. Sal goes to work _____ 7:30.

4. Our break is _____ 3:00 _____ 3:15.

5. Dan goes to school _____ Monday and Wednesday.

6. Peter gets up _____ 8:30 _____ Saturday.

7. Min goes to sleep _____ 11:00 _____ Friday.

8. Sue works _____ 8:00 _____ 4:00.

9. We eat lunch _____ 12:00 _____ 1:00 every day.

10. Sam goes to work _____ 9:00 _____ Thursday.

**B** Write sentences. Use *from, to, at,* or *on.*

1. They work / Monday / Friday. _They work from Monday to Friday._

2. English class is / 5:00 _____

3. Class is over / 7:00 _____

4. I go to school / Saturday _____

5. They eat breakfast / 7:30 _____

6. Our break is / 12:15 / 12:30 _____

7. Kate and Joe work / 8:30 / 4:00 _____

8. I study / Saturday _____

9. I work / Tuesday / Friday _____

10. We work / 12:00 / 5:00 / Saturday _____

_____

# CONVERSATION REVIEW

**ROLE-PLAY.**

**Student A**
Ask about Student B's schedule.
Then answer Student B's questions.

**Student B**
Answer Student A's questions.
Then ask about Student A's schedule.

**A:** When do you work?

**B:** I work from _____ to _____.

**A:** When do you go to school?

**B:** I go to school on _____.

**A:** What time do you _____?

**B:** I _____ at _____.

## Student A

### My Schedule

| Sunday | Monday | Tuesday | Wednesday | Thursday | Friday | Saturday |
|---|---|---|---|---|---|---|
| go to library 12:00 | get up 7:00 work 9:00–5:00 play soccer 6:00–7:30 | get up 6:00 work 8:30–4:30 go to school 6:00–8:00 | get up 7:00 work 9:00–5:00 | get up 7:00 work 9:00–5:00 | get up 7:00 work 9:00–5:00 | get up 9:00 go to school 12:00–3:00 meet friends 6:00 go to sleep 11:00 |

## Student B

### My Schedule

| Sunday | Monday | Tuesday | Wednesday | Thursday | Friday | Saturday |
|---|---|---|---|---|---|---|
| get up 10:00 meet friends 12:00 | get up 9:00 go to school 10:00–5:00 | get up 6:00 work 8:00–4:00 | get up 7:00 work 9:00–5:00 | get up 7:00 work 9:00–5:00 play soccer 6:00–7:30 | get up 8:00 work 10:00–4:00 go to school 6:00–8:00 | get up 9:00 work 11:00–6:00 go to sleep 11:30 |

# LIFE SKILLS AND WRITING REVIEW

## 1 LIFE SKILLS: Read and write a weekly schedule

**A** Ask and answer the questions.

1. When do you work?
2. When do you go to school?
3. When is your break?
4. When do you study English?
5. When do you meet friends?

**B** Write your information in the schedule.

### My Schedule

| Sunday | Monday | Tuesday | Wednesday | Thursday | Friday | Saturday |
|--------|--------|---------|-----------|----------|--------|----------|
|        |        |         |           |          |        |          |

## 2 WRITE ABOUT YOURSELF

Complete the sentences.

1. I work _____.
2. I go to class _____.
3. My break is _____.
4. I study English _____.
5. I meet friends _____.

**Unit Review:** Go back to page 47. Which unit goals can you check off?

# 4

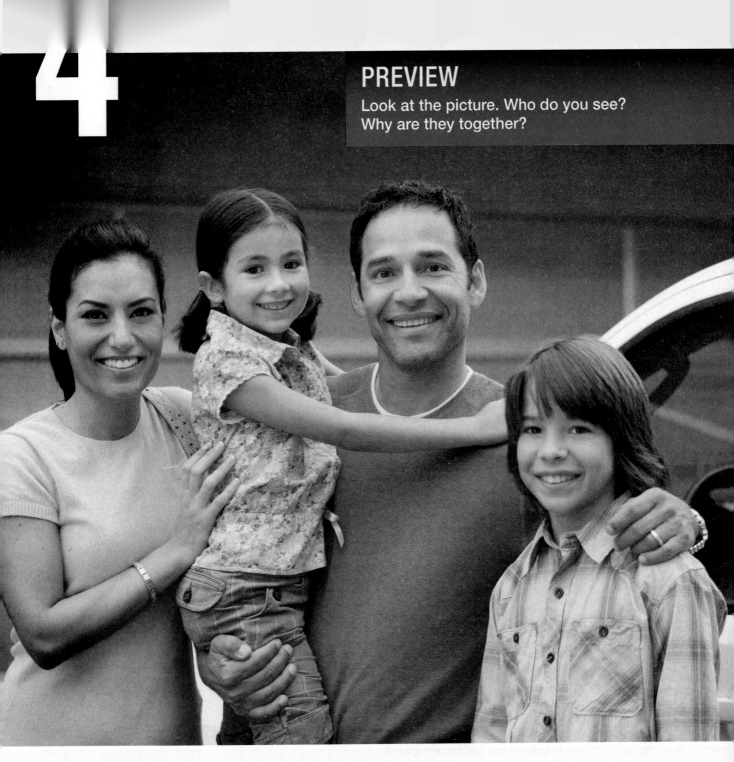

## PREVIEW

Look at the picture. Who do you see?
Why are they together?

## UNIT GOALS

- [ ] Identify family members
- [ ] Say who is in your family
- [ ] Talk about chores at home
- [ ] Say months of the year
- [ ] Write dates

- [ ] Read and write about home and work
- [ ] **Life skills:** Fill out a form
- [ ] **English at work:** Ask about someone's family

# That's my brother.

## 1 VOCABULARY: Family members

**A** Look at the pictures. What do you see?

▶ Listen and point. Listen and repeat.

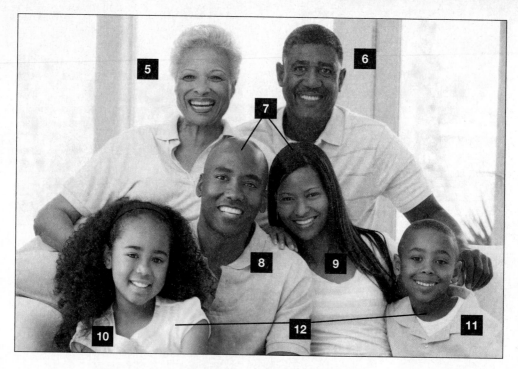

**B** ▶ Listen and read. Listen and repeat.

| | | | |
|---|---|---|---|
| **1.** sister | **2.** brother | **3.** husband | **4.** wife |
| **5.** grandmother | **6.** grandfather | **7.** parents | **8.** father |
| **9.** mother | **10.** daughter | **11.** son | **12.** children |

## 2 CONVERSATION

**A** ▶ Listen. Listen and repeat.

**A:** Who's that?

**B:** That's my brother.

**A:** What's his name?

**B:** Sam.

**A:** Who's that?

**B:** That's my sister.

**A:** What's her name?

**B:** Her name is Tina.

**B** Practice the conversation.

## Show what you know!

**1. TALK ABOUT IT.** Show pictures of your family. Ask and answer.

A: Who's that?
B: That's my _____.
A: What's _____ name?
B: _____ name is _____.

**2. WRITE ABOUT IT.** Write the names of your family members.

My sister is Emma.
My mother is Angela.

I can identify family members. ■                    I need more practice. ■

# I have two sisters and one brother.

## 1 CONVERSATION

**A** ▶ Listen. Listen and repeat.

A: Do you have any sisters or brothers?
B: Yes. I have two sisters and one brother.
A: That's nice. Do you have any children?
B: No, I don't.

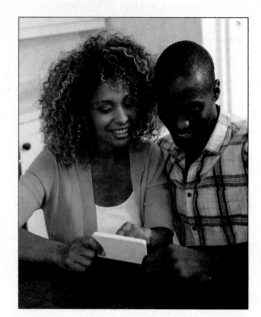

**B** Circle *Yes* or *No*.

1. The woman has two sisters.          Yes     No
2. The woman has two brothers.         Yes     No
3. The woman has children.             Yes     No

**C** Practice the conversation.

## 2 READING

**A** ▶ Listen and read.

Hi, I'm Marta. This is my family. That's my husband. His name is Pedro. My parents are Linda and Roberto. I have two sons, Ernesto and Tino. I have one daughter. Her name is Ana.

Pedro    Marta    Linda    Roberto

Tino    Ernesto         Ana

**B** Complete the sentences about Marta's family.

1. Pedro is her _____.
2. Ana is her _____.
3. Linda is her _____.
4. Ernesto and Tino are her _____.
5. Roberto and Linda are her _____.

# Say Who Is in Your Family

## 3 GRAMMAR: Singular and plural

**A** ▶ Listen and read. Listen and repeat.

| Singular | Plural |
|----------|--------|
| one brother | two brothers |
| a sister | three sisters |
| one son | two sons |
| a daughter | three daughters |
| one parent | two parents |
| one child | two children |

**B** Match.

_b_ **1.** my brother Tom and my brother Mark     **a.** my parents

____ **2.** my son and daughter     **b.** my brothers

____ **3.** my mother and father     **c.** my sisters

____ **4.** my sister Sue and my sister Mary     **d.** my children

## Show what you know!

**1. TALK ABOUT IT.** Ask and answer.

A: Do you have any sisters or brothers?
B: _____.
A: Do you have any children?
B: _____.

**2. WRITE ABOUT IT.** Write sentences.

I have one brother.
I have two daughters.

I can say who is in my family. ■     I need more practice. ■

# Do you vacuum?

## 1 VOCABULARY: Household chores

**A** Look at the pictures. What do you see?

▶ Listen and point. Listen and repeat.

**B** ▶ Listen and read. Listen and repeat.

| | | |
|---|---|---|
| **1.** do the laundry | **2.** wash the dishes | **3.** make dinner |
| **4.** clean the house | **5.** vacuum | **6.** take out the garbage |

**C** What household chores do you do? Read the sentences. Circle *Yes* or *No*.

**1.** I vacuum.               Yes     No
**2.** I do the laundry.        Yes     No
**3.** I make dinner.           Yes     No
**4.** I wash the dishes.       Yes     No
**5.** I clean the house.       Yes     No
**6.** I take out the garbage.  Yes     No

# Talk About Chores at Home

## 2 CONVERSATION

**A** ▶ Listen. Listen and repeat.

**A:** Do you vacuum?
**B:** Yes, I do.
**A:** Do you make dinner?
**B:** No, I don't.

**B** Practice the conversation.

## 3 GRAMMAR: *Yes / No* questions

| Questions | Answers |
|---|---|
| Do you wash the dishes? | **Yes,** I do. |
| Do you clean the house? | **No,** I don't. |
| Do you vacuum? | **Yes,** I do. |
| Do you do the laundry? | **No,** I don't. |

> End a question with a question mark.

**Write the questions.**

1. you / vacuum     <u>Do you vacuum?</u>
2. you / do the laundry   _____
3. you / make dinner   _____
4. you / wash the dishes   _____
5. you / clean the house   _____
6. you / take out the garbage   _____

---

### Show what you know!

**1. TALK ABOUT IT.** Ask about household chores.

A: Do you _____?
B: _____, I _____.

**2. WRITE ABOUT IT.** What chores do you do?

I do the dishes.

I clean the house.

---

I can talk about chores at home. ☐      I need more practice. ☐

## 1 VOCABULARY: Months and seasons

**A** ▶ Listen and point. Listen and repeat.

**Months**

| January | February | March | April | May | June |
|---|---|---|---|---|---|
| S M T W T F S | S M T W T F S | S M T W T F S | S M T W T F S | S M T W T F S | S M T W T F S |
| 1 2 3 4 5 | 1 2 | 1 2 | 1 2 3 4 5 6 | 1 2 3 4 | 1 |
| 6 7 8 9 10 11 12 | 3 4 5 6 7 8 9 | 3 4 5 6 7 8 9 | 7 8 9 10 11 12 13 | 5 6 7 8 9 10 11 | 2 3 4 5 6 7 8 |
| 13 14 15 16 17 18 19 | 10 11 12 13 14 15 16 | 10 11 12 13 14 15 16 | 14 15 16 17 18 19 20 | 12 13 14 15 16 17 18 | 9 10 11 12 13 14 15 |
| 20 21 22 23 24 25 26 | 17 18 19 20 21 22 23 | 17 18 19 20 21 22 23 | 21 22 23 24 25 26 27 | 19 20 21 22 23 24 25 | 16 17 18 19 20 21 22 |
| 27 28 29 30 31 | 24 25 26 27 28 | 24/31 25 26 27 28 29 30 | 28 29 30 | 26 27 28 29 30 31 | 23/30 24 25 26 27 28 29 |

| July | August | September | October | November | December |
|---|---|---|---|---|---|
| S M T W T F S | S M T W T F S | S M T W T F S | S M T W T F S | S M T W T F S | S M T W T F S |
| 1 2 3 4 5 6 | 1 2 3 | 1 2 3 4 5 6 7 | 1 2 3 4 5 | 1 2 | 1 2 3 4 5 6 7 |
| 7 8 9 10 11 12 13 | 4 5 6 7 8 9 10 | 8 9 10 11 12 13 14 | 6 7 8 9 10 11 12 | 3 4 5 6 7 8 9 | 8 9 10 11 12 13 14 |
| 14 15 16 17 18 19 20 | 11 12 13 14 15 16 17 | 15 16 17 18 19 20 21 | 13 14 15 16 17 18 19 | 10 11 12 13 14 15 16 | 15 16 17 18 19 20 21 |
| 21 22 23 24 25 26 27 | 18 19 20 21 22 23 24 | 22 23 24 25 26 27 28 | 20 21 22 23 24 25 26 | 17 18 19 20 21 22 23 | 22 23 24 25 26 27 28 |
| 28 29 30 31 | 25 26 27 28 29 30 31 | 29 30 | 27 28 29 30 31 | 24 25 26 27 28 29 30 | 29 30 31 |

**B** ▶ Listen. Circle the month.

1. November       December
2. July           June
3. October        November
4. January        July
5. March          May
6. August         April

> Start months with a capital letter.

**C** Look at the pictures. What do you see?

▶ Listen and point. Listen and repeat.

**Seasons**

**spring**          **summer**          **fall**          **winter**

# Say Months of the Year

**D** Write the months.

| Seasons in the United States | | | |
|---|---|---|---|
| **Spring** | **Summer** | **Fall** | **Winter** |
| | | | |
| | | | |
| | | | |

## 2 CONVERSATION

**A** ▶ Listen. Listen and repeat.

**A:** What's your favorite season?
**B:** Summer.
**A:** That's nice. My favorite season is spring.

**B** Practice the conversation.

**C** WORK TOGETHER. Make new conversations.

**A:** What's your favorite season?
**B:** _____.
**A:** That's nice. My favorite season is _____.

### Show what you know!

**1. TALK ABOUT IT.** What's your favorite month?

A: What's your favorite month?
B: My favorite month is _____.

**2. WRITE ABOUT IT.** What's your favorite season?

My favorite season is fall.

---

I can say months of the year. ■                    I need more practice. ■

# 5 Write Dates

## What is today's date?

# 1 VOCABULARY: Dates

**A** Put the months in the correct order. Write the numbers. Then write the words.

____ November ____ December ____ January ____ March

____ April ____ July ____ February ____ August

____ October ____ May ____ September ____ June

1. _____ 7. _____

2. _____ 8. _____

3. _____ 9. _____

4. _____ 10. _____

5. _____ 11. _____

6. _____ 12. _____

**B** ▶ Listen and point. Listen and repeat.

| September 28, 1998 | January 2, 2018 | June 20, 2010 |
|---|---|---|
| 9/28/1998 | 1/2/2018 | 6/20/2010 |
| April 19, 2008 | December 22, 1987 | March 15, 2025 |
| 4/19/2008 | 12/22/1987 | 3/15/2025 |

**C** Match the dates.

1. January 1, 2017      5/15/1993

2. April 12, 2020      5/31/2014

3. May 15, 1993      1/1/2017

4. August 27, 2000      8/27/2000

5. May 31, 2014      4/12/2020

**D** ▶ Listen. Circle the date.

1. 2/23/1994      3/23/1994

2. 7/14/2015      7/4/2015

3. 9/22/2009      9/2/2009

4. 1/29/2011      1/11/2019

5. 9/17/1974      9/7/1974

# Write Dates

**E** Write the dates. Use numbers.

1. September 2, 2010   _____
2. April 12, 2013      _____
3. May 21, 2012        _____
4. September 2, 1999   _____
5. October 7, 2021     _____
6. July 30, 1988       _____

## 2 CONVERSATION

**A** ▶ Listen. Listen and repeat.

**A:** What is today's date?
**B:** April 9, 2019.
**A:** Thanks.

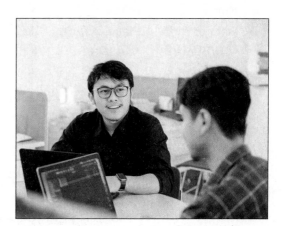

**B** Practice the conversation.

**C** WORK TOGETHER. Make new conversations.

**A:** What is today's date?
**B:** _____.
**A:** Thanks.

---

### Show what you know!

**1. WRITE ABOUT IT.** Write dates. Use words and numbers.

*February 28, 2019*
*2/28/2019*

**2. TELL THE CLASS.** Look at your partner's dates. Say the dates.

---

I can write dates. ■                                    I need more practice. ■

# What is your teacher's name?

## 1 READING

**A** ▶ Listen and read.

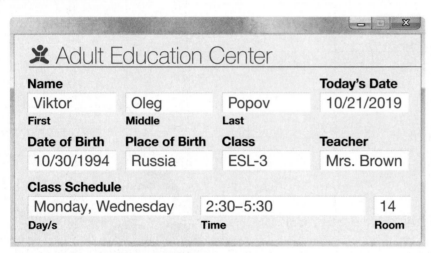

**Adult Education Center**

| Name | | | Today's Date |
|---|---|---|---|
| Viktor | Oleg | Popov | 10/21/2019 |
| First | Middle | Last | |

| Date of Birth | Place of Birth | Class | Teacher |
|---|---|---|---|
| 10/30/1994 | Russia | ESL-3 | Mrs. Brown |

**Class Schedule**

| Monday, Wednesday | 2:30–5:30 | | 14 |
|---|---|---|---|
| Day/s | Time | | Room |

**date of birth: 2/18/2019**

**B** Complete the sentences about Viktor.

1. Viktor is a _____.
2. Viktor's last name is _____.
3. He is from _____.
4. Viktor's date of birth is _____.
5. His teacher is _____.
6. His class is _____.
7. His class is on Monday and _____.
8. His class is over at _____.

# 2 WRITING

**A** Answer the questions.

1. What is your first name? _____
2. What is your last name? _____
3. What is your date of birth? _____
4. Where are you from? _____
5. What class are you in? _____
6. What is your teacher's name? _____
7. What day is your class? _____
8. What time does your class start? _____
9. What time does your class end? _____
10. What room is your class in? _____

**B** Fill out the form. Use your information in Exercise A.

**C** **WORK TOGETHER.** Read your classmate's form. Is the form complete?

**D** GO ONLINE.

1. Find an application form online.
2. Fill out the form.

I can fill out a form. ☐                    I need more practice. ☐

# Read and Write About Home and Work

## Lucas and Carla are married.

**1 LISTENING**

**A** Look at each picture. What do you see?

**B** ▶ Listen to the story.

# Read and Write About Home and Work

## 2 READING

**A** ▶ Read and listen.

> Lucas and Carla are married. Lucas is Carla's husband. Carla is Lucas's wife.
> In their native country, men go to work.
> In their native country, women do the household chores.
> In the United States, Carla and Lucas go to work.
> They both do household chores. Lucas washes the dishes.
> Lucas goes to the supermarket, too.

**B** Circle *Yes* or *No*.

| | | |
|---|---|---|
| **1.** Lucas is Carla's husband. | Yes | No |
| **2.** In the United States, Carla goes to work. | Yes | No |
| **3.** In their native country, women go to work. | Yes | No |
| **4.** In the United States, Lucas does household chores. | Yes | No |

## 3 WRITING

**A** MAKE CONNECTIONS. Talk about work and household chores in your native country.

**1.** Do men and women go to work?

**2.** Do women do household chores?

**3.** Do men do household chores? What household chores do they do?

**B** Complete the sentences.

**1.** In my native country, _____ work.

**2.** _____ do household chores.

**3.** In the United States, _____ work.

**4.** _____ do household chores.

**C** WORK TOGETHER. Read your sentences.

| I can read and write about home and work. ■ | I need more practice. ■ |
|---|---|

# Lesson 8
## Mara is at work.

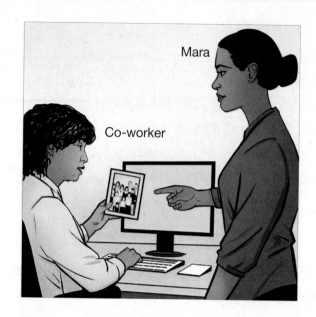

Mara

Co-worker

## 1 READING

Mara is an assistant.
She works in an office.
She asks her co-worker about her family.

## 2 CONVERSATION AT WORK

**A** Complete the conversation. Write the correct words.

**Mara:** Is that your family?

**Co-worker:** Yes, it is. That's my _____ and three sisters.

| brother | sister |
|---|---|

**Mara:** _____?

| That's nice | Who's that |
|---|---|

**Co-worker:** That's my _____.

| grandmother | grandparents |
|---|---|

**Mara:** You have a nice family.

**Co-worker:** _____!

| You're welcome | Thank you |
|---|---|

**B** Practice the conversation.

**C** Role-play the conversation with new information.

I can ask about someone's family. ■       I need more practice. ■

**A** Write the months of the year in the correct order.

1. _____          7. _____
2. _____          8. _____
3. _____          9. _____
4. _____          10. _____
5. _____          11. _____
6. _____          12. _____

**B** ▶ Listen and check your answers.

**C** Read the calendar. Write the dates in words and numbers.

April 5, 2020
4/5/2020

**April 2020**

| S | M | T | W | T | F | S |
|---|---|---|---|---|---|---|
|   |   |   | 1 | 2 | 3 | 4 |
| 5 | 6 | 7 | 8 | 9 | 10 | 11 |
| 12 | 13 | 14 | 15 | 16 | 17 | 18 |
| 19 | 20 | 21 | 22 | 23 | 24 | 25 |
| 26 | 27 | 28 | 29 | 30 |   |   |

**D** Write the chores.

clean the house            do the laundry            make dinner
take out the garbage       vacuum                    wash the dishes

1. _____

2. _____

3. _____

4. _____

5. _____

6. _____

## A Complete the chart.

| Singular | Plural |
|---|---|
| sister | *sisters* |
| parent | |
| | brothers |
| daughter | |
| | sons |
| grandmother | |
| child | |

## B Complete the conversations. Write *his* or *her*.

**1. A:** That's my brother.
  **B:** What's _____ his _____ name?

**2. A:** That's my grandmother.
  **B:** What's _____ name?

**3. A:** That's my husband.
  **B:** What's _____ name?

**4. A:** I have one sister.
  **B:** What's _____ name?

## C Complete the conversations.

**1. A:** Do you wash the dishes?
  **B:** Yes, _____ I do _____.

**2. A:** _____ you take out the garbage?
  **B:** No, I don't.

**3. A:** Do you do the laundry?
  **B:** Yes, I _____.

**4. A:** Do you _____ dinner?
  **B:** Yes, I do.

**5. A:** _____ you clean the house?
  **B:** No, I _____.

**6. A:** _____ you vacuum?
  **B:** Yes, I _____.

**ROLE-PLAY.**

Show pictures of your family. Or talk about this picture.

**Student A**
Ask about Student B's family.

**Student B**
Ask about Student A's family.

**A:** Who's that?

**B:** That's my _____.

**A:** What's _____ name?

**B:** _____.

# LIFE SKILLS AND WRITING REVIEW

## 1 LIFE SKILLS: Fill out a form

Fill out the form.

**Student Information Form**

T L C
The Language Center

○ Mr.   ○ Mrs.   ○ Miss   ○ Ms.

**Name**

| | | | **Today's Date** |

First          Middle          Last

**Date of Birth    Place of Birth    Class        Teacher**

**Class Schedule**

Day/s                        Time                        Room

## 2 WRITE ABOUT YOURSELF

Complete the sentences.

1. My name is _____.
2. I'm from _____.
3. I'm in _____.
4. My teacher is _____.
5. I go to English class on _____.
6. Class starts at _____.

**Unit Review:** Go back to page 65. Which unit goals can you check off?

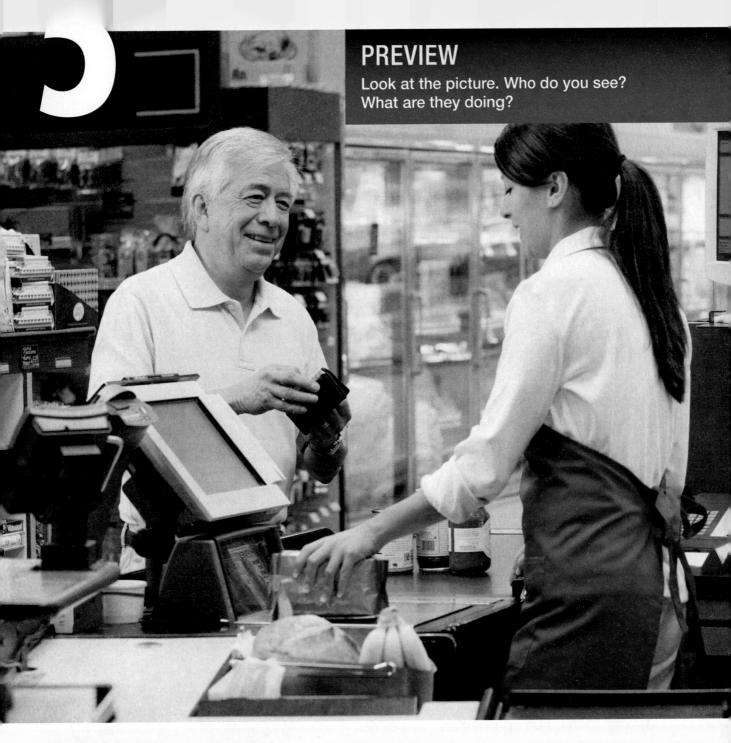

**PREVIEW**

Look at the picture. Who do you see?
What are they doing?

# UNIT GOALS

- ☐ Make change with U.S. coins
- ☐ Make change with U.S. bills
- ☐ Ask where things are in a store
- ☐ Ask for and say prices
- ☐ Read and write about shopping

- ☐ **Life skills:** Read a receipt
- ☐ **English at work:** Answer a customer's questions

# Make Change with U.S. Coins

## Do you have change for a dollar?

### 1 VOCABULARY: U.S. coins

**A** Look at the pictures. What do you see?

▶ Listen and point. Listen and repeat.

**B** ▶ Listen and read. Listen and repeat.

| | | |
|---|---|---|
| **1.** a penny | **2.** a nickel | **3.** a dime |
| **4.** a quarter | **5.** a half-dollar | |

**C** MAKE CONNECTIONS. Take out your coins. Count the coins. Tell your partner.

*I have three quarters.*

### 2 CONVERSATION

**A** ▶ Listen. Listen and repeat.

**A:** Excuse me. Do you have change for a dollar?

**B:** Yes. I have two quarters and five dimes. Here you go.

**A:** Thanks.

**B** Practice the conversation.

**C** Look at the pictures. Complete the sentences.

1. **A:** Do you have change for a dollar?
   **B:** Yes. I have _____.

2. **A:** Do you have change for a dollar?
   **B:** Yes. I have _____.

3. **A:** Do you have change for a quarter?
   **B:** Yes. I have _____.

4. **A:** Do you have change for a quarter?
   **B:** Yes. I have _____.

**D** ▶ Listen and check your answers. Listen and repeat.

## Show what you know!

**1. WRITE ABOUT IT.** Complete the conversation.

A: Do you have change for a _____?
B: Yes. I have _____. Here you go.
A: Thanks.

**2. TELL THE CLASS.** Role-play your conversation with a partner.

I can make change with U.S. coins. ■            I need more practice. ■

## 1 VOCABULARY: U.S. bills

**A** Look at the pictures. What do you see?

▶ Listen and point. Listen and repeat.

**1**

**2**

**3**

**4**

**5**

**6**

**B** ▶ Listen and read. Listen and repeat.

| | |
|---|---|
| **1.** one dollar | **2.** five dollars |
| **3.** ten dollars | **4.** twenty dollars |
| **5.** fifty dollars | **6.** one hundred dollars |

**C** **WORK TOGETHER.** Say a bill. Your partner points to the picture.

# Make Change with U.S. Bills

## 2 CONVERSATION

**A** ▶ Listen. Listen and repeat.

A: Excuse me. Do you have change for a ten?
B: Yes. I have a five and five ones. Here you go.
A: Great.

**B** Practice the conversation.

**C** Look at the pictures. Complete the sentences.

1. A: Do you have change for a five?
   B: Yes. I have _____.

2. A: Do you have change for a twenty?
   B: Yes. I have _____.

3. A: Do you have change for a fifty?
   B: Yes. I have _____.

4. A: Do you have change for a hundred?
   B: Yes. I have _____.

**D** ▶ Listen and check your answers. Listen and repeat.

## Show what you know!

**1. WRITE ABOUT IT.** Complete the conversation.

A: Excuse me. Do you have change for a _____?
B: Yes. I have _____. Here you go.
A: Great.

**2. TALK ABOUT IT.** Practice your conversation with a partner.

I can make change with U.S. bills. ■          I need more practice. ■

# Ask Where Things Are in a Store

## Where is the soap?

### 1 VOCABULARY: Drugstore items

**A** Look at the pictures. What do you see?

▶ Listen and point. Listen and repeat.

**1**

**2**

**3**

**4**

**5**

**6**

**7**

**8**

**9**

**10**

**11**

**12**

**B** ▶ Listen and read. Listen and repeat.

| | | | |
|---|---|---|---|
| **1.** soap | **2.** deodorant | **3.** toilet paper | **4.** paper towels |
| **5.** toothpaste | **6.** shaving cream | **7.** batteries | **8.** light bulbs |
| **9.** shampoo | **10.** aspirin | **11.** razors | **12.** tissues |

**C** **WORK TOGETHER.** Point to a picture. Your partner says the word.

## 2 GRAMMAR: *Where is, where are*

**Where is** the soap?          **Where are** the razors?

**Where is** the aspirin?          **Where are** the tissues?

**A** Complete the sentences. Write *is* or *are*.

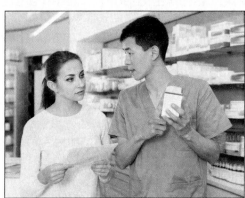

1. Where _____is_____ the shampoo?
2. Where _____ the paper towels?
3. Where _____ the shaving cream?
4. Where _____ the light bulbs?
5. Where _____ the batteries?

**B** ▶ Listen and check your answers. Listen and repeat.

## Show what you know!

**1. WRITE ABOUT IT.** Look at the signs. Write questions.

Where is the _____?

Where are the _____?

| Aisle **1** | Aisle **2** | Aisle **3** | Aisle **4** |
|---|---|---|---|
| deodorant | toothpaste | paper towels | light bulbs |
| shaving cream | shampoo | toilet paper | aspirin |
| razors | soap | tissues | batteries |

**2. TALK ABOUT IT.** Ask and answer your questions.

A: Where is the soap?

B: Aisle 2.

I can ask where things are in a store. ■          I need more practice. ☐

# Ask for and Say Prices

## How much is the toothpaste?

## 1 VOCABULARY: Prices

**A** ▶ Listen and point. Listen and repeat.

¢ = cents

15¢    27¢    49¢    55¢    75¢    82¢    99¢

**B** ▶ Listen. Write the prices.

1. _____    2. _____    3. _____

4. _____    5. _____    6. _____

**C** ▶ Listen and point. Listen and repeat.

$ = dollars

$1.50    $5.39    $10.25    $22.70    $36.00    $66.83    $93.99

**D** ▶ Listen. Write the prices.

1. _____    2. _____    3. _____

4. _____    5. _____    6. _____

7. _____    8. _____    9. _____

**E** WORK TOGETHER. Say a price. Your partner writes the price.

## 2 CONVERSATION

**A** ▶ Listen. Listen and repeat.

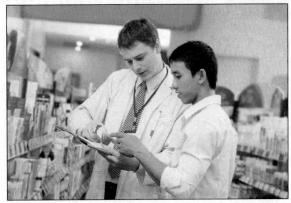

**A:** Excuse me. How much is the toothpaste?
**B:** It's $3.99.
**A:** How much are the batteries?
**B:** They're $4.50.
**A:** Thanks.

**B** Practice the conversation.

**C** **WORK TOGETHER.** Look at the pictures. Make new conversations.

**A:** Excuse me. How much is the _____?
**B:** It's _____.
**A:** How much are the _____?
**B:** They're _____.
**A:** Thanks.

| $1.99 | $2.99 | $3.00 | $7.99 | $4.59 | $3.19 |

### Show what you know!

**1. WRITE ABOUT IT.** Write a new price for each item.

1. deodorant _____
2. soap _____
3. shampoo _____
4. shaving cream _____
5. aspirin _____
6. batteries _____

**2. TALK ABOUT IT.** Walk around the room. Ask about each item.

*How much is the deodorant?*

I can ask for and say prices. ☐                    I need more practice. ☐

# Swipe your card.

## 1 VOCABULARY

**A** Look at the pictures. What do you see?

**1** Credit Card 🌐
1234 5678 9012 3456
Bo Mi Kim  GOOD THRU 11/23

**2**

**3**

**4**

**5**

**6**

**7** 253

**B** ▶ Listen and read. Listen and repeat.

| | | | |
|---|---|---|---|
| **1.** a card | **2.** swipe your card | **3.** insert your card | **4.** tap OK |
| **5.** sign your name | **6.** remove your card | **7.** enter your PIN | |

**C** Write the words on the correct lines.

| enter your PIN | insert | sign | swipe | tap |
|---|---|---|---|---|

## 2 READING

**A** Read the receipt.

**Family Drugstore**

Date> 3/4/19

| | |
|---|---|
| 1 Shampoo | |
| 1 Soap | $5.79 |
| 1 Tissues | 2.99 |
| 1 Razors | 3.79 |
| 1 Shaving cream | 5.99 |
| 1 Batteries | 6.25 |
| | 6.99 |

Transaction Total:

| 6 items | Subtotal | $31.80 |
|---|---|---|
| | Tax | 2.23 |
| | Total | $34.03 |

Paid by: Credit card $34.03

**B** Circle *Yes* or *No*.

| | | | |
|---|---|---|---|
| 1. | The name of the store is Drugstore. | Yes | No |
| 2. | The date on the receipt is March 4, 2019. | Yes | No |
| 3. | The person is buying five items. | Yes | No |
| 4. | The person is paying with a card. | Yes | No |

## 3 WRITING

**A** Complete the sentences.

1. The shampoo is _____ .
2. The tissues are _____ .
3. The razors are _____ .
4. The shaving cream is _____ .
5. The tax is _____ .
6. The total is _____ .

**B** GO ONLINE.

1. Find an online drugstore.
2. Write the prices of items you want to buy. Add the prices. What is your total?

I can read a receipt. ☐                    I need more practice. ☐

## 1 LISTENING

**A** Look at each picture. What do you see?

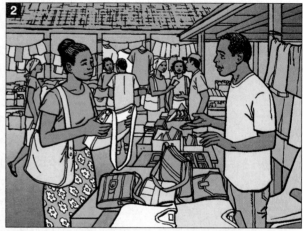

**B** ▶ Listen to the story.

## 2 READING

**A** ▶ Read and listen.

This is Edna. In her native country, she shops at a market.
She talks about the price. She asks for a better price.
She is happy.
In the United States, Edna shops in a big store.
Each item has one price.
Edna pays a good price in the United States, too. She buys things on sale.

**B** Circle *Yes* or *No*.

| | | | |
|---|---|---|---|
| **1.** Edna is from the United States. | Yes | No | |
| **2.** In Edna's native country, she shops at a big store. | Yes | No | |
| **3.** In Edna's native country, she asks for a better price. | Yes | No | |
| **4.** In the United States, Edna shops at a big store. | Yes | No | |
| **5.** In the United States, Edna buys things on sale. | Yes | No | |

## 3 WRITING

**A** **MAKE CONNECTIONS.** Talk about shopping in your native country.

**1.** Do people shop at markets? Do they shop in big stores?
**2.** Do people ask for a better price?
**3.** Do people pay good prices?

**B** Complete the sentences.

**1.** In my native country, people _____.
**2.** In the United States, people _____.
**3.** In _____, people pay a good price.
**4.** In _____, each item has one price.

**C** **WORK TOGETHER.** Read your sentences.

I can read and write about shopping. ■         I need more practice. ■

# Fatima is at work.

**Customer** **Fatima**

## 1 READING

Fatima is a cashier.
She works in a store.
She makes change for a customer.

## 2 CONVERSATION AT WORK

**A** Complete the conversation. Write the correct words.

**Customer:** _____. How much are
the batteries?

**Fatima:** Let me see. _____ $4.79.

**Customer:** OK. I need new batteries.

**Fatima:** The total is $4.95.

**Customer:** _____ change for a ten?

**Fatima:** Yes, I do.

**Customer:** Great. _____.

**Fatima:** Thank you. Here is your

_____.

| | |
|---|---|
| Excuse me | Great |
| It's | They're |
| Do you have | I have |
| No, I don't | Here you go |
| change | total |

**B** Practice the conversation.

**C** Role-play the conversation with new information.

I can answer a customer's questions. ■          I need more practice. ■

## A. Write the name of the coin. Write the amount.

| dime | nickel | quarter | 5¢ | 25¢ |
| half dollar | penny | 1¢ | 10¢ | 50¢ |

_____   _____   _____   _____   _____

_____   _____   _____   _____   _____

## B. Point to a bill. Say the amount.

## C. WORK TOGETHER. Ask for change.

**A:** Excuse me. Do you have change for _____?

**B:** Yes. I have _____. Here you go.

**A:** Thanks.

**A** Complete the sentences. Write *Where is* or *Where are*.

1. _____Where is_____ the deodorant?
2. _____ the shaving cream?
3. _____ the tissues?
4. _____ the shampoo?
5. _____ the batteries?
6. _____ the razors?

**B** Complete the sentences. Write *How much is* or *How much are*.

1. ___How much is___ the aspirin?
2. _____ the toilet paper?
3. _____ the soap?
4. _____ the paper towels?
5. _____ the toothpaste?
6. _____ the light bulbs?

**C** Answer the questions from Exercise B.

1. The aspirin _____is $3.79._____     $3.79

2. The toilet paper _____     $3.49

3. The soap _____     $1.99

4. The paper towels _____     $4.99

5. The toothpaste _____     $5.79

6. The light bulbs _____     $3.99

## ROLE-PLAY.

**Student A**
Look at the pictures.
Ask Student B where something is.

**Student B**
Answer Student A's question.

**A:** Excuse me. Where _____ the _____?
**B:** Aisle _____.
**A:** Thanks.

| Aisle 2 | Aisle 1 | Aisle 5 |
| $1.99 | $4.99 | $5.50 |

| Aisle 4 | Aisle 6 | Aisle 3 |
| $3.99 | $5.79 | $1.99 |

**Student B**
Look at the pictures.
Ask Student A how much something is.

**Student A**
Answer Student B's question.

**B:** Excuse me. How much _____ the _____?
**A:** It's _____. (They're _____.)
**B:** Thanks.

## 1 LIFE SKILLS: Read a receipt

**A** Circle the correct word.

| | | |
|---|---|---|
| 1. Swipe your _____. | card | PIN |
| 2. _____ your card. | Tap | Insert |
| 3. _____ OK. | Tap | Sign |
| 4. _____ your name. | Sign | Insert |
| 5. Enter your _____. | PIN | card |
| 6. _____ your card. | Tap | Remove |
| 7. _____ with a card. | Pay | Sign |

**B** Read the receipt. Answer the questions.

### CDS Drugstore

```
Date> 8/11/19

1 Shampoo            $4.79
1 Soap               1.89
1 Tissues            3.99
1 Razors             5.50
1 Paper towels       4.25

Transaction Total:

5 items      Subtotal $20.42
             Tax        1.43
             Total    $21.85

Paid by: Credit card $21.85
```

1. How much is the shampoo?

   _____

2. How much are the paper towels?

   _____

3. What is the date on the receipt?

   _____

4. How much is the total?

   _____

## 2 WRITE ABOUT YOURSELF

Complete the sentences.

1. My name is _____.
2. I shop at _____.
3. I buy _____.
4. I pay with _____.

**Unit Review:** Go back to page 85. Which unit goals can you check off?

# 8

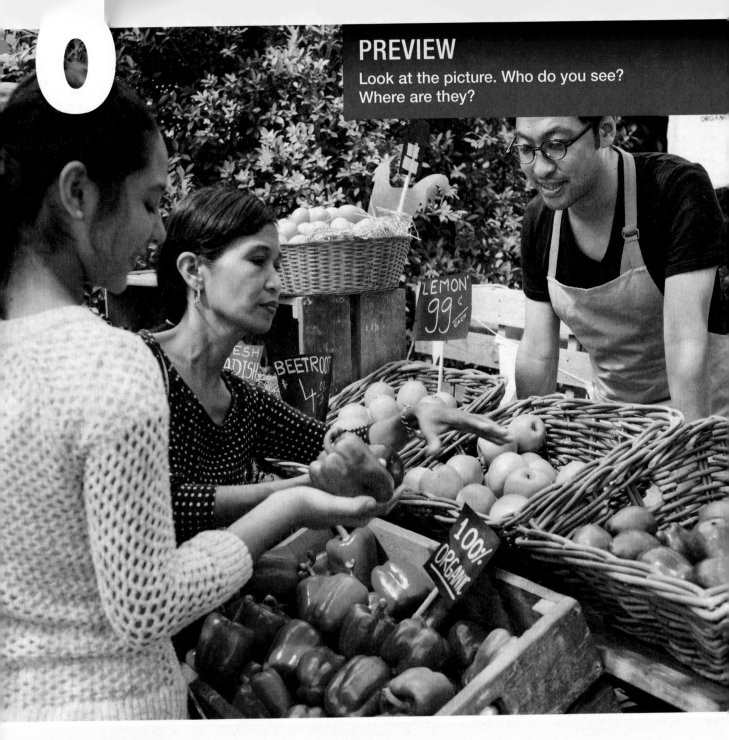

## PREVIEW

Look at the picture. Who do you see?
Where are they?

LEMON
99¢
EACH

ESH
ADISH

BEETROOT
4

100%
ORGANIC

## UNIT GOALS

- ☐ Talk about vegetables
- ☐ Say what you like and don't like
- ☐ Say what someone likes and doesn't like
- ☐ Ask what someone needs

- ☐ Read a menu and order food
- ☐ Read and write about eating
- ☐ **Life skills:** Read an ad; Make a shopping list
- ☐ **English at work:** Do an inventory

# Talk About Vegetables

## Do we need vegetables?

### 1 VOCABULARY: Vegetables

**A** Look at the pictures. What do you see?

▶ Listen and point. Listen and repeat.

**1**

**2**

**3**

**4**

**5**

**6**

**7**

**8**

**9**

**B** ▶ Listen and read. Listen and repeat.

| | | |
|---|---|---|
| **1.** tomatoes | **2.** carrots | **3.** cucumbers |
| **4.** onions | **5.** peppers | **6.** lettuce |
| **7.** potatoes | **8.** mushrooms | **9.** peas |

**C** **WORK TOGETHER.** Point to a picture. Your partner says the word.

# Talk About Vegetables

## 2 CONVERSATION

**A** ▶ Listen. Listen and repeat.

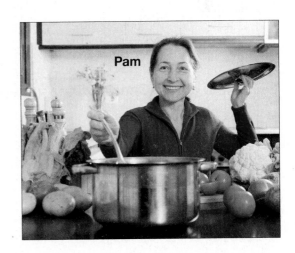

**A:** Hi. I'm at the store. Do we need vegetables?
**B:** Yes. We need tomatoes and carrots.
**A:** OK. Do we need onions?
**B:** No. We have onions.

**B** Practice the conversation.

**C** **WORK TOGETHER.** Make new conversations.

**A:** Hi. I'm at the store. Do we need vegetables?
**B:** Yes. We need _____ and _____.
**A:** OK. Do we need _____?
**B:** No. We have _____.

**D** ▶ Listen and read.

Hi, I'm Pam. It's time to make vegetable soup!
I have tomatoes, onions, peas, and potatoes.
I need mushrooms and carrots.

Pam

**E** Circle *Yes* or *No*.

| | | |
|---|---|---|
| 1. Pam has mushrooms. | Yes | No |
| 2. She needs tomatoes. | Yes | No |
| 3. She has onions. | Yes | No |
| 4. She needs carrots. | Yes | No |

## Show what you know!

**1. WRITE ABOUT IT.** What vegetables do you have at home?

I have _____.

**2. TALK ABOUT IT.** Tell your partner.

I have peas and carrots.

I can talk about vegetables. ■       I need more practice. ■

Unit 6, Lesson 1  **105**

# Lesson 2   Do you like vegetables?

## 1 CONVERSATION

**A** ▶ Listen. Listen and repeat.

**A:** Do you like vegetables?
**B:** I like tomatoes. I don't like onions.
What about you?
**A:** I like peppers. I don't like carrots.

**B** ▶ Listen again. Check (✓) the vegetables they like.

☐ tomatoes
☐ onions
☐ peppers
☐ carrots

**C** ▶ Listen again. Check (✓) the vegetables they don't like.

☐ tomatoes
☐ onions
☐ peppers
☐ carrots

**D** Practice the conversation.

**E** WORK TOGETHER. Make new conversations.

**A:** Do you like vegetables?
**B:** I like _____.
I don't like _____. What about you?
**A:** I like _____.
I don't like _____.

## 2 GRAMMAR: *Like, don't like*

| | |
|---|---|
| I **like** tomatoes. | I **don't like** onions.<br>I **do not like** onions. |
| You **like** lettuce. | You **don't like** carrots.<br>You **do not like** carrots. |
| Luz and Pavel **like** potatoes. | They **don't like** peas.<br>They **do not like** peas. |
| John and I **like** cucumbers. | We **don't like** mushrooms.<br>We **do not like** mushrooms. |

**Complete the sentences. Use *like* and *don't like*.**

> do not = don't

 **1.** I  *like cucumbers* _____ .

 **2.** Carlos and Susan _____ .

 **3.** We _____ .

 **4.** You _____ .

 **5.** I _____ .

## Show what you know!

**1. WRITE ABOUT IT.** Write about food you like and don't like.

I like _____, _____, and _____.

I don't like _____, _____, or _____.

| I can say what I like and don't like. ☐ | I need more practice. ☐ |
|---|---|

# Say What Someone Likes and Doesn't Like

## Does your daughter like fruit?

## 1 VOCABULARY: Fruit

**A** Look at the pictures. What do you see?

▶ Listen and point. Listen and repeat.

**B** ▶ Listen and read. Listen and repeat.

| | | |
|---|---|---|
| **1.** apples | **2.** cherries | **3.** mangoes |
| **4.** oranges | **5.** pears | **6.** strawberries |
| **7.** bananas | **8.** peaches | **9.** grapes |

**C** Write three fruits you like.

_____   _____   _____

**D** WORK TOGETHER. Tell your partner.

I like _____.

# Say What Someone Likes and Doesn't Like

## 2 CONVERSATION

**A** ▶ Listen. Listen and repeat.

A: Does your daughter like fruit?
B: She likes apples. She doesn't like pears.

**B** Practice the conversation.

## 3 GRAMMAR: *Likes, doesn't like*

| | |
|---|---|
| My daughter **likes** apples. | She **doesn't like** pears.<br>She **does not like** pears. |
| My son **likes** oranges. | He **doesn't like** bananas.<br>He **does not like** bananas. |
| Tara **likes** pears. | She **doesn't like** mangoes.<br>She **does not like** mangoes. |

does not = doesn't

**Complete the sentences.**

1. My mother ___likes___ grapes.
   <sub>like</sub>

2. My teacher _____ peaches.
   <sub>not / like</sub>

3. He _____ apples.
   <sub>not / like</sub>

4. She _____ bananas.
   <sub>like</sub>

### Show what you know!

1. **TALK ABOUT IT.** Talk to your classmates. Complete the chart.

   I like _____. I don't like _____.

| Name | Likes | Doesn't Like |
|---|---|---|
| | | |
| | | |
| | | |

2. **WRITE ABOUT IT.** Write sentences.

   Olga likes apples. She doesn't like pears.

I can say what someone likes and doesn't like. ☐     I need more practice. ☐

# Ask What Someone Needs

# Do you need anything from the store?

## 1 VOCABULARY: Amounts

▶ Listen and point. Listen and repeat.

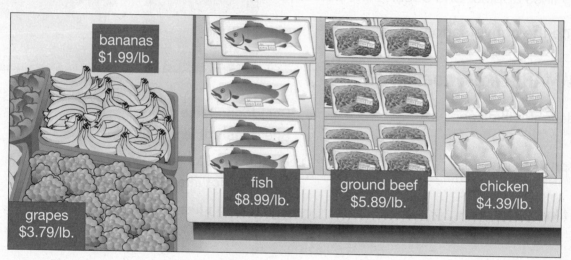

bananas
$1.99/lb.

fish
$8.99/lb.

ground beef
$5.89/lb.

chicken
$4.39/lb.

grapes
$3.79/lb.

lb. = pound
lbs. = pounds

## 2 CONVERSATION

**A** ▶ Listen. Listen and repeat.

**A:** Do you need anything from the store?
**B:** Yes. I need one pound of grapes and two pounds of ground beef.

**B** Practice the conversation.

**C** **WORK TOGETHER.** Look at the shopping lists. Make new conversations.

**A:** Do you need anything from the store?
**B:** Yes. I need _____ and _____.

Shopping List 1

2 lbs. of grapes
1 lb. of bananas

Shopping List 2

1 lb. of fish
2 lbs. of ground beef

Shopping List 3

3 lbs. of bananas
4 lbs. of chicken

# Ask What Someone Needs

## 3 VOCABULARY: Containers

▶ Listen and point. Listen and repeat.

**a gallon of milk**

**a loaf of bread**

**a box of cereal**

**a dozen eggs**

**a bag of rice**

**a can of soup**

| Singular | | Plural |
|---|---|---|
| bag | → | bags |
| box | → | boxes |
| can | → | cans |
| dozen | → | two dozen |
| gallon | → | gallons |
| loaf | → | loaves |

## 4 CONVERSATION

**A** ▶ Listen. Listen and repeat.

**A:** What do we need from the store?
**B:** We need a bag of rice and two dozen eggs.

**B** Practice the conversation.

**C** **WORK TOGETHER.** Look at the pictures. Make new conversations.

**A:** What do we need from the store?
**B:** We need _____ and _____.

**Conversation 1**

**Conversation 2**

**Conversation 3**

### Show what you know!

**1. TALK ABOUT IT.** What do you need from the store?

I need _____.

**2. WRITE ABOUT IT.** Write sentences.

Ann needs a pound of grapes.

I can ask what someone needs. ■      I need more practice. ■

# Lesson 5

## How much is bread?

## 1 READING

**A** ▶ Listen and read.

**Shop Mart Weekly Specials**

Loaf of bread
$1.79

One dozen eggs
$1.29

Chicken
$1.99/lb.

Tomato soup
79¢
Buy one,
get one free

Cereal
$4.25

Bananas 49¢/lb.

**B** Circle the answer.

1. How much is bread?

   $1.79 a loaf                    $1.79 a pound

2. How much is one dozen eggs?

   99¢                            $1.29

3. How much is chicken?

   $1.99 each                     $1.99 a pound

4. How much is a can of tomato soup?

   $1.79                          79¢

5. How much is cereal?

   $4.25 a box                    $4.25 a pound

6. How much are two pounds of bananas?

   98¢                            $1.49

## 2 WRITING

**A** Look at the pictures. Write the shopping lists.

2 dozen eggs
1 pound of chicken
2 cans of soup

**B** **WORK TOGETHER.** Read your lists to your classmate.

**C** GO ONLINE.

1. Find food prices on your favorite supermarket's website or app.
2. Write the foods you need and the prices you see.

| Food | Price |
|------|-------|
| _____ | _____ |
| _____ | _____ |
| _____ | _____ |

I can read an ad. ☐                                    I need more practice. ☐

## 1 VOCABULARY: Food on a menu

**A** ▶ Listen and point. Listen and repeat.

a tuna fish sandwich   a chicken sandwich   a cheeseburger   a baked potato

a green salad   a fruit salad   French fries   rice

pancakes   eggs and toast   cereal

iced tea   juice   coffee   tea

**B** **WORK TOGETHER.** Say a food. Your partner points to the picture.

# Read a Menu and Order Food

## 2 CONVERSATION

**A** ▶ Listen. Listen and repeat.

**A:** Are you ready to order?

**B:** Yes. I'd like a tuna fish sandwich, a green salad, and an iced tea.

**A:** Anything else?

**B:** No, thank you.

**B** Practice the conversation.

### Show what you know!

**1. WRITE ABOUT IT.** Look at the menu. Write foods you'd like.

I'd like _____, _____, and _____.

| Breakfast | | French fries | $3.75 |
|---|---|---|---|
| pancakes | $4.50 | baked potato | $2.50 |
| eggs and toast | $4.00 | rice | $2.25 |
| cereal | $3.00 | green salad | $3.50 |
| | | fruit salad | $4.00 |
| **Lunch and Dinner** | | | |
| cheeseburger | $4.50 | **Drinks** | |
| chicken sandwich | $4.00 | juice | $3.00 |
| tuna fish sandwich | $5.00 | coffee | $2.25 |
| | | tea | $2.25 |
| | | iced tea | $2.00 |

**2. TELL THE CLASS.** Order food from the menu.

I'd like a cheeseburger, a fruit salad, and juice.

I can read a menu and order food. ■          I need more practice. ■

## 1 | LISTENING

**A** Look at each picture. What do you see?

**B** ▶ Listen to the story.

# Read and Write About Eating

## 2 READING

**A** ▶ Read and listen.

This is Tran. In his native country, most people eat with chopsticks.
Many children eat with their hands.
This is Riko. In her native country, many people drink soup.
In the United States, most people eat with a fork, knife, and spoon.
They eat sandwiches and French fries with their hands.

**B** Circle *Yes* or *No*.

| | | |
|---|---|---|
| 1. Tran eats with chopsticks. | Yes | No |
| 2. In Tran's native country, many children eat with their hands. | Yes | No |
| 3. In Riko's native country, people eat soup with a spoon. | Yes | No |
| 4. In the United States, most people use a knife and fork. | Yes | No |
| 5. In the United States, people eat sandwiches with chopsticks. | Yes | No |

## 3 WRITING

**A** MAKE CONNECTIONS. Talk about eating in your native country.

1. Do people eat with chopsticks?
2. Do people eat with their hands?
3. Do people eat with a knife, fork, and spoon?

**B** Complete the sentences.

1. In my native country, most people eat with _____.
2. Children eat with _____.
3. In the United States, most people eat with _____.

**C** WORK TOGETHER. Read your sentences.

I can read and write about eating. ■          I need more practice. ■

# English at Work: Do an Inventory

## Sara is at work.

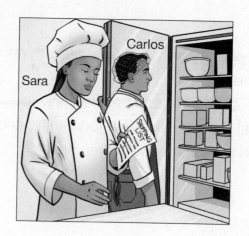

Sara

Carlos

SHOPPING LIST

## 1 READING

Sara is a cook.
She works in a restaurant.
She does an inventory with Carlos.

## 2 CONVERSATION AT WORK

**A** Complete the conversation. Write the correct words.

| | |
|---|---|
| **Carlos:** | _____ ground beef? |
| **Sara:** | Yes, we need _____ of ground beef. |
| **Carlos:** | OK, got it. What about vegetables? What do we need? |
| **Sara:** | Let's see. _____ carrots, potatoes, and lettuce. |
| **Carlos:** | Anything else? |
| **Sara:** | Oh! We need three _____ of milk. |

| | |
|---|---|
| Do you like | Do we need |
| four gallons | four pounds |

| | |
|---|---|
| We need | She needs |

| | |
|---|---|
| gallons | loaves |

**B** Practice the conversation.

**C** Role-play the conversation with new information.

I can do an inventory. ■

I need more practice. ■

# VOCABULARY REVIEW

**A** Look at the picture. Write the foods.

**B** Circle the word that does not belong in each group.

| | | |
|---|---|---|
| **1.** apples | cucumbers | pears |
| **2.** lettuce | carrots | oranges |
| **3.** chicken | ground beef | lemons |
| **4.** rice | bread | apples |
| **5.** mushrooms | milk | onions |
| **6.** cherries | eggs | grapes |
| **7.** cereal | potatoes | tomatoes |
| **8.** peas | mangoes | strawberries |

**C** WORK TOGETHER. Write one word for each quantity.

**1.** a pound of _____

**2.** a bag of _____

**3.** a box of _____

**4.** a loaf of _____

**5.** a dozen _____

# GRAMMAR REVIEW

**A** Complete the sentences. Write *like* or *likes*.

1. I _____like_____ carrots.
2. Tara _____ peas.
3. Tom and Sue _____ apples.
4. We _____ bread.
5. Jim _____ milk.
6. They _____ vegetable soup.
7. Kara _____ pancakes.

**B** Complete the sentences. Write *don't like* or *doesn't like*.

1. Bob and Tran ____don't like____ juice.
2. I _____ onions.
3. Kate _____ eggs.
4. We _____ bananas.
5. Jack _____ eggs.
6. They _____ grapes.
7. She _____ bread.

**C** Complete the conversations. Write *I like* or *I'd like*.

1. **A:** Do you like fruit?
   **B:** Yes. ____I like____ apples.
2. **A:** Are you ready to order?
   **B:** Yes. _____ pancakes.
3. **A:** Do you like vegetables?
   **B:** _____ peas.
4. **A:** Are you ready to order?
   **B:** _____ a cheeseburger, please.

**ROLE-PLAY.**

**Student A**
You are a server.
Ask for the customer's lunch order.
Write the order.

**Student B**
You are the customer.
Look at the menu.
Order lunch.

| **Breakfast** | | **French fries** | $3.75 |
|---|---|---|---|
| pancakes | $4.50 | baked potato | $2.50 |
| eggs and toast | $4.00 | rice | $2.25 |
| cereal | $3.00 | green salad | $3.50 |
| | | fruit salad | $4.00 |
| **Lunch and Dinner** | | | |
| cheeseburger | $4.50 | **Drinks** | |
| chicken sandwich | $4.00 | juice | $3.00 |
| tuna fish sandwich | $5.00 | coffee | $2.25 |
| | | tea | $2.25 |
| | | iced tea | $2.00 |

**A:** Are you ready to order?

**B:** Yes. I'd like _____, _____, and _____.

**A:** Anything else?

**B:** _____.

**Switch roles.**

**B:** Are you ready to order?

**A:** Yes. I'd like _____, _____, and _____.

**B:** Anything else?

**A:** _____.

## 1 LIFE SKILLS: Make a shopping list

**A** ▶ Listen. Complete the shopping list.

_____ of rice

_____ eggs

a pound of _____

_____ of chicken

**B** MAKE CONNECTIONS. What do you need? Write a shopping list.

## 2 WRITE ABOUT YOURSELF

Complete the sentences.

1. I shop for fruits and vegetables at _____.
2. I shop for bread at _____.
3. I shop for meat at _____.
4. I also buy _____.
5. My favorite restaurant is _____.
   I like _____ there.

**Unit Review:** Go back to page 103. Which unit goals can you check off?

# 7 Apartment for Rent

## PREVIEW

Look at the picture. Who do you see?
Where are they?

## UNIT GOALS

- [ ] Identify rooms in a home
- [ ] Talk about a home
- [ ] Ask about furniture and appliances
- [ ] Give an address

- [ ] Read and write about moving
- [ ] **Life skills:** Address an envelope
- [ ] **English at work:** Talk about apartments

# 1 Identify Rooms in a Home

## I have a new apartment.

### 1 VOCABULARY: Rooms in a home

**A** Look at the picture. What do you see?

▶ Listen and point. Listen and repeat.

**B** ▶ Listen and read. Listen and repeat.

| | | |
|---|---|---|
| **1.** bedroom | **2.** bathroom | **3.** closet |
| **4.** living room | **5.** dining room | **6.** kitchen |
| **7.** laundry room | **8.** basement | **9.** garage |

**C** **WORK TOGETHER.** Point to a room. Your partner names it.

# Identify Rooms in a Home

## 2 CONVERSATION

**A** ▶ Listen. Listen and repeat.

A: Guess what? I have a new apartment.
B: Really? What's it like?
A: It has a kitchen, a living room, and one bedroom.
B: It sounds great!

**B** Practice the conversation.

**C** WORK TOGETHER. Look at the pictures. Make new conversations.

A: Guess what? I have a new apartment.
B: Really? What's it like?
A: It has _____.
B: It sounds great!

**Conversation 1**

**Conversation 2**

## Show what you know!

**1. WRITE ABOUT IT.** Write the rooms in your home.

My home has _____, _____, and _____.

**2. TELL THE CLASS.** Talk about the rooms in your home.

My home has a kitchen, two bedrooms, and one bathroom.

| I can identify rooms in a home. ☐ | I need more practice. ☐ |

# Talk About a Home

## Can you tell me about the apartment?

## 1 VOCABULARY: Words to describe rooms

▶ Listen and point. Listen and repeat.

| sunny | new | large | small |

## 2 CONVERSATION

**A** ▶ Listen. Listen and repeat.

**A:** Can you tell me about the apartment for rent?
**B:** There is a sunny bedroom, a new kitchen, and a large living room.
**A:** It sounds nice.

**B** Practice the conversation.

**C** WORK TOGETHER. Look at the apartments. Make new conversations.

**A:** Can you tell me about the apartment for rent?
**B:** There is a _____, a _____, and a _____.
**A:** It sounds nice.

### Conversation 1

### Conversation 2

# Talk About a Home

## 3 GRAMMAR: *There is, there are*

**There is** a kitchen.
**There is** a living room.

**There are** two bedrooms.
**There are** two bathrooms.

**A** Complete the sentences. Write *There is* or *There are*.

I like my home. _____*There are*_____ six rooms. _____ two

small bedrooms. _____ a living room. _____

a new kitchen. _____ a large bathroom. _____

a laundry room in the basement.

**B** Circle *Yes* or *No*.

| | | |
|---|---|---|
| **1.** There are three rooms. | Yes | No |
| **2.** The bedrooms are small. | Yes | No |
| **3.** The kitchen is old. | Yes | No |
| **4.** There is a laundry room. | Yes | No |

## Show what you know!

**1. WRITE ABOUT IT.** Write about your home.

There is _____.

There are _____.

**2. TALK ABOUT IT.** Talk about your home.

There is a sunny living room.
There are two small bedrooms.

# Ask About Furniture and Appliances

## Is there a refrigerator?

## 1 VOCABULARY: Furniture and appliances

**A** Look at the pictures. What do you see?

▶ Listen and point. Listen and repeat.

**B** ▶ Listen and read. Listen and repeat.

| | | | |
|---|---|---|---|
| **1.** sink | **2.** dishwasher | **3.** stove | **4.** refrigerator |
| **5.** toilet | **6.** shower | **7.** bed | **8.** dresser |
| **9.** lamp | **10.** sofa | **11.** chair | **12.** table |
| **13.** washing machine | **14.** dryer | | |

**C** What is in your home?

_____   _____   _____

_____   _____   _____

**D** MAKE CONNECTIONS. Tell your classmate what is in your home.

# Ask About Furniture and Appliances

## 2 CONVERSATION

**A** ▶ Listen. Listen and repeat.

**A:** I have some questions about the apartment. Is there a refrigerator?

**B:** Yes, there is.

**A:** Are there any lamps?

**B:** No, there aren't.

**B** Practice the conversation.

## 3 GRAMMAR: *Is there, are there*

| Is there a dishwasher? | Yes, there is. | No, there isn't. <br> No, there's not. |
|---|---|---|
| Are there any beds? | Yes, there are. | No, there aren't. <br> No, there are not. |

**A** Complete the questions and the answers.

> there is = there's
> is not = isn't
> are not = aren't

1. **A:** _____Is there_____ a stove?
   **B:** Yes, _____.

2. **A:** _____ any chairs?
   **B:** Yes, _____.

3. **A:** _____ any lamps?
   **B:** No, _____.

4. **A:** _____ a washing machine?
   **B:** No, _____.

**B** ▶ Listen and check your answers. Listen and repeat.

### Show what you know!

**1. TALK ABOUT IT.** Ask about your partner's home.

Is there a _____?
Are there any _____?

**2. WRITE ABOUT IT.** Write about your partner's home.

There is a washing machine.
There aren't any dressers.

| I can ask about furniture and appliances. ☐ | I need more practice. ☐ |
|---|---|

# Give an Address

## What's the address?

### 1 VOCABULARY: Addresses

**A** ▶ Listen and point. Listen and repeat.

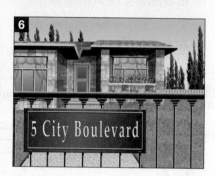

**B** ▶ Listen. Circle the address.

1. 207 John Lane          270 John Lane
2. 15 City Street          51 City Street
3. 1460 Third Avenue          1640 Third Avenue
4. 40 Park Drive          60 Park Drive
5. 309 Sun Boulevard          319 Sun Boulevard

**C** ▶ Listen. Complete the addresses.

1. _____ Sandy Boulevard
2. _____ West Avenue
3. _____ Main Street
4. _____ Jones Road
5. _____ North Drive
6. _____ Town Lane

# Give an Address

## 2 CONVERSATION

**A** ▶ Listen. Listen and repeat.

**A:** I'm looking for an apartment.
**B:** Oh! There's an apartment for rent on my street.
**A:** What's the address?
**B:** It's 1630 River Street.
**A:** How much is the rent?
**B:** It's $900 a month.

**B** Circle *Yes* or *No*.

1. There is an apartment for rent on her street.     Yes     No
2. The address is 1260 River Street.     Yes     No
3. The rent is $900 a month.     Yes     No

**C** Practice the conversation.

### Show what you know!

**1. TALK ABOUT IT.** Read the ads. Make new conversations.

| Conversation 1 | Conversation 2 | Conversation 3 |
|---|---|---|
| ● ● ● | ● ● ● | ● ● ● |
| 1 bedroom | 3 bedrooms | 2 bedrooms |
| 658 River Drive | 1920 Park Lane | 19 Bank Street |
| $975/month | $1,300/month | $1,125/month |

A: I'm looking for an apartment.
B: Oh! There's an apartment for rent on my street.
A: What's the address?
B: It's _____.
A: How much is the rent?
B: It's _____.

**2. WRITE ABOUT IT.** Write one of your conversations.

I can give an address. ■                    I need more practice. ■

# Life Skills: Address an Envelope

# Who is the letter from?

## 1 VOCABULARY

Write the abbreviation.

| Apt. | Ave. | Blvd. | Dr. | Ln. | Rd. | St. |
| --- | --- | --- | --- | --- | --- | --- |

1. Street _____
2. Avenue _____
3. Drive _____
4. Lane _____
5. Road _____
6. Boulevard _____
7. Apartment _____

## 2 READING

**A** Read the envelope.

return address — 
Dave Clark
9106 River Rd. Apt. 115
Chicago, IL 60623

street address — Tina Smith
7754 Park Ave.
Chicago, IL 60647

city —
state —
ZIP code —

**B** Circle the answers.

| | | |
| --- | --- | --- |
| 1. Who is the letter from? | Tina Smith | Dave Clark |
| 2. What is the return address? | 9106 River Rd. | 7754 Park Ave. |
| 3. Who is the letter to? | Tina Smith | Dave Clark |
| 4. What is Tina's ZIP code? | 60647 | 60326 |
| 5. What is Dave's ZIP code? | 60623 | 60547 |

## 3 WRITING

**A** Answer the questions.

1. What's your first and last name? _____
2. What's your street address? _____
3. What's your city and state? _____
4. What's your ZIP code? _____

**B** GO ONLINE.

1. Find a business online. Find the business's address. Answer the questions.

   **a.** What's the name of the business?

   _____

   **b.** What's the street address?

   _____

   **c.** What's the city and state?

   _____

   **d.** What's the ZIP code?

   _____

2. Address an envelope to the business. Write your address for the return address.

| | |
|---|---|
| | |

I can address an envelope. ▪          I need more practice. ▪

# Read and Write About Moving

## This is Pilar.

### 1 LISTENING

**A** Look at each picture. What do you see?

**B** ▶ Listen to the story.

# Read and Write About Moving

## 2 READING

### A ▶ Read and listen.

This is Pilar. She is 21 years old. She is single.

Pilar lives with her sister and her sister's husband.

Pilar has a good job. She works in an office.

Pilar wants to live with her friends. In the United States, many single people live with friends.

Pilar's parents are not happy. In their native country, single people live with their families.

### B Circle *Yes* or *No*.

| | | |
|---|---|---|
| **1.** Pilar lives with her parents. | Yes | No |
| **2.** Pilar has a job. | Yes | No |
| **3.** Pilar wants to live with her friends. | Yes | No |
| **4.** Pilar's parents want Pilar to live with her friends. | Yes | No |
| **5.** In the United States, many single people live with friends. | Yes | No |

## 3 WRITING

### A MAKE CONNECTIONS. Talk about where people live in your native country.

1. Do single people live with their families?
2. Do single people live with friends?

### B Complete the sentences.

1. In my native country, many single people live _____.
2. In the United States, many single people live _____.

### C WORK TOGETHER. Read your sentences.

| | |
|---|---|
| I can read and write about moving. ■ | I need more practice. ☐ |

# English at Work: Talk About Apartments

## Vera is at work.

## 1 READING

Vera is a building manager.
She works in an apartment building.
She helps people rent apartments.

## 2 CONVERSATION AT WORK

**A** Complete the conversation. Write the correct words.

| | | |
|---|---|---|
| **Vera:** | Good morning. Can I help you? | |

**Customer:** Good morning. I'm looking for a two-bedroom apartment.

**Vera:** OK. I have an apartment _____ on River Street.

| for sale | for rent |
|---|---|

**Customer:** What's it like?

**Vera:** _____ two bedrooms, a kitchen, and a living room.

| There is | There are |
|---|---|

**Customer:** It sounds great! _____?

**Vera:** It's $1,150 a month.

| How much is the rent | What's the address |
|---|---|

**Customer:** What's the _____?

**Vera:** It's 32 River Street.

| kitchen | address |
|---|---|

**B** Practice the conversation.

**C** Role-play the conversation with new information.

| I can talk about apartments. ■ | I need more practice. ■ |
|---|---|

# VOCABULARY REVIEW

**A** ▶ **LISTEN. Listen and repeat.**

| | | | | |
|---|---|---|---|---|
| bathroom | bed | bedroom | chair | dining room |
| dryer | kitchen | lamp | living room | refrigerator |
| sink | sofa | stove | table | washing machine |

**B** Look at Exercise A. Circle the furniture and appliances. Underline the rooms.

**C** Look at the picture. Write the words.

1. _____

2. _____

3. _____

4. _____

# GRAMMAR REVIEW

**A** Complete the sentences. Write *There is* or *There are*.

I have a great apartment. _____There is_____ a large living room. _____
two sunny bedrooms. _____ a new kitchen. _____ a table in
the kitchen. _____ four chairs. _____ a laundry room in the
basement. _____ a bathroom. _____ a shower in the bathroom.
_____ two sinks.

**B** Complete the conversations.

1. **A:** _____Is there_____ a laundry room?
   **B:** No, _____.
2. **A:** _____ any dressers?
   **B:** Yes, _____.
3. **A:** _____ any chairs?
   **B:** No, _____.
4. **A:** _____ a washing machine?
   **B:** No, _____.
5. **A:** _____ a dishwasher?
   **B:** Yes, _____.
6. **A:** _____ a garage?
   **B:** No, _____.
7. **A:** _____ any closets?
   **B:** Yes, _____.
8. **A:** _____ any beds?
   **B:** No, _____.

## ROLE-PLAY.

**Student A**
There is an apartment with furniture for rent.
Ask about the apartment. Ask about:

| | |
|---|---|
| the address | a refrigerator |
| the rent | chairs |
| a stove | a sunny living room |

**A:** Can you tell me about the apartment? What's the address?

**B:** It's _____.

**A:** How much is the rent?

**B:** It's _____ a month.

**A:** Is there _____?

**B:** _____.

**A:** Are there any _____?

**B:** _____.

**Student B**
Look at the apartment.
Answer Student A's questions.

Apartment for rent
3420 River Street
$1,050/month

**Student B**
There is an apartment with furniture for rent.
Ask about the apartment. Ask about:

| | |
|---|---|
| the address | a large bathroom |
| the rent | two bedrooms |
| a sofa | lamps |

**B:** Can you tell me about the apartment? What's the address?

**A:** It's _____.

**B:** How much is the rent?

**A:** It's _____ a month.

**B:** Is there _____?

**A:** _____.

**B:** Are there any _____?

**A:** _____.

**Student A**
Look at the apartment.
Answer Student B's questions.

# LIFE SKILLS AND WRITING REVIEW

## 1 LIFE SKILLS: Read an ad

**A** Read the ads.

<table>
<tr>
<td>

**FOR RENT**
1 bedroom apartment
New stove, refrigerator
Living room has sofa and chairs

$995/month
Call Robert 613-555-8714

**A**
</td>
<td>

**FOR RENT**
Apartment in house
2 bedrooms
Garage
Laundry room in basement
$1,200/month
Call Rosa 312-555-9312

**B**
</td>
</tr>
</table>

**B** Read the sentences. Match the sentences with the ads. Write *A* or *B*.

1. There is furniture. _____
2. There are two bedrooms. _____
3. There is a new stove. _____
4. There is a laundry room. _____
5. The rent is $995 a month. _____
6. There is a garage. _____

## 2 WRITE ABOUT YOURSELF

Complete the sentences.

1. My favorite room is _____.
2. There is _____.
3. There are _____.

**Unit Review:** Go back to page 123. Which unit goals can you check off?

# 8 Let's Go Shopping

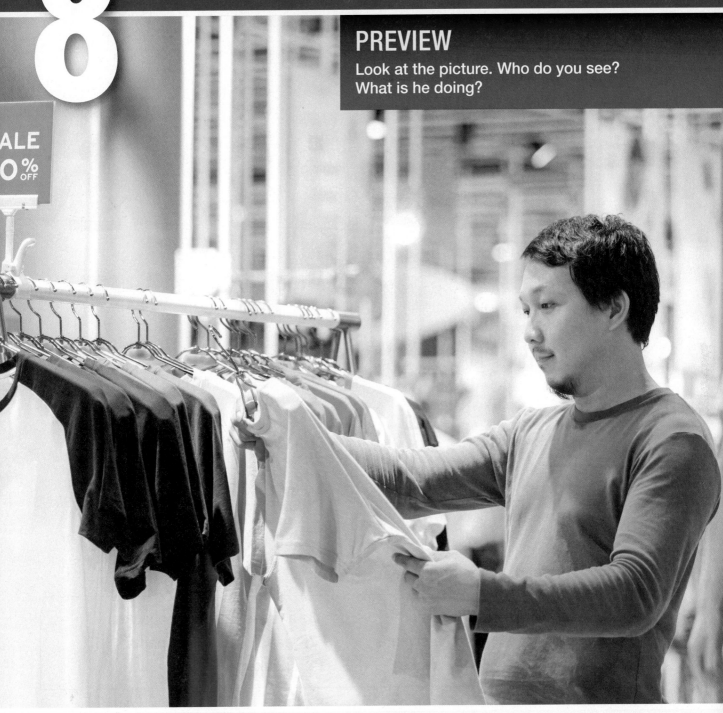

## PREVIEW

Look at the picture. Who do you see?
What is he doing?

ALE
0% OFF

## UNIT GOALS

☐ Identify clothing you need
☐ Ask for clothing sizes
☐ Describe clothing
☐ Return clothing to a store

☐ Read and write about clothing at a wedding
☐ **Life skills:** Read store ads
☐ **English at work:** Help a customer return clothes

# Identify Clothing You Need

# I need a new jacket.

## 1 VOCABULARY: Clothing

**A** Look at the pictures. What do you see?

▶ Listen and point. Listen and repeat.

**B** ▶ Listen and read. Listen and repeat.

| | | | |
|---|---|---|---|
| **1.** a T-shirt | **2.** a skirt | **3.** a dress | **4.** a jacket |
| **5.** a shirt | **6.** a sweater | **7.** jeans | **8.** pants |
| **9.** socks | **10.** shoes | **11.** sneakers | |

**C** **MAKE CONNECTIONS.** Look at your classmates. What clothing do you see?

# Identify Clothing You Need

## 2 CONVERSATION

**A** ▶ Listen. Listen and repeat.

**A:** Let's go shopping! I need a new jacket.
**B:** OK. I need new shoes.

**B** Practice the conversation.

**C** **WORK TOGETHER.** Look at the pictures. Make new conversations.

**A:** Let's go shopping! I need a new _____.
**B:** OK. I need new _____.

### Conversation 1

### Conversation 2

### Conversation 3

---

## Show what you know!

**1. WRITE ABOUT IT.** What clothing do you need?

I need a new _____.

I need new _____.

**2. TALK ABOUT IT.** What clothing do you need?

I need a new dress.

I need new shoes.

---

I can identify clothing I need. ■                    I need more practice. ■

# Lesson 2 · Ask for Clothing Sizes

## Do you have this shirt in large?

### 1 VOCABULARY: Clothing sizes

▶ Listen and point. Listen and repeat.

**small** S  **medium** M  **large** L  **extra large** XL

### 2 CONVERSATION

**A** ▶ Listen. Listen and repeat.

A: Can I help you?

B: Do you have this shirt in large?

A: Yes. Here you go.

B: Do you have these pants in size 12?

A: No, I'm sorry. We don't.

**B** Practice the conversation.

**C** WORK TOGETHER. Look at the pictures. Make new conversations.

A: Can I help you?

B: Do you have this _____ in large?

A: Yes. Here you go.

B: Do you have these _____ in size 12?

A: No, I'm sorry. We don't.

**Conversation 1**

**Conversation 2**

**Conversation 3**

## Ask for Clothing Sizes

### 3 GRAMMAR: *This, that, these, those*

Do you have **this** shirt in large?

No, but we have **that** shirt in large.

Do you have **these** shirts in small?

No, but we have **those** shirts in small.

**A** Complete the sentences. Write *this* or *these*.

1. Do you have _____*this*_____ jacket in extra large?
2. Do you have _____ shoes in size 8?
3. We have _____ sweaters in small.
4. We have _____ dress in size 10.
5. We have _____ shirt in medium.

**B** Complete the sentences. Write *that* or *those*.

1. Do you have _____*those*_____ socks in a small?
2. Do you have _____ skirt in large?
3. We have _____ pants in size 16.
4. We have _____ T-shirts in extra large.
5. We have _____ shirt in size 6.

### Show what you know!

**1. WRITE ABOUT IT.** Make a new conversation.

A: Do you have this _____ in _____?
B: No, I'm sorry. We don't. We have that _____ in _____.
A: Do you have these _____ in _____?
B: No, I'm sorry. We don't. We have those _____ in _____.

**2. TALK ABOUT IT.** Practice your conversation.

I can ask for clothing sizes. ■                    I need more practice. ■

## Describe Clothing

# What does she have on?

## 1 VOCABULARY: Colors

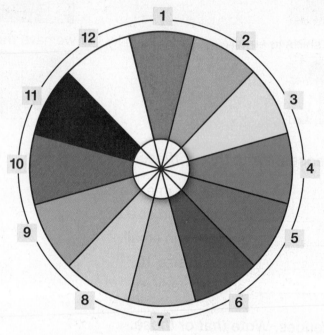

**A** ▶ Listen and point. Listen and repeat.

**B** ▶ Listen and read. Listen and repeat.

| | | | |
|---|---|---|---|
| **1.** red | **2.** orange | **3.** yellow | **4.** green |
| **5.** blue | **6.** purple | **7.** pink | **8.** beige |
| **9.** gray | **10.** brown | **11.** black | **12.** white |

**C** Write your answers.

1. What color is your favorite jacket?
   My favorite jacket is _____.

2. What color are your favorite pants?
   My favorite pants are _____.

3. What color are your favorite shoes?
   My favorite shoes are _____.

4. What color is your favorite T-shirt?
   My favorite T-shirt is _____.

5. What is your favorite color?
   My favorite color is _____.

**D** **WORK TOGETHER.** Ask your classmate the questions in Exercise C.

# Describe Clothing

## 2 CONVERSATION

**A** ▶ Listen. Listen and repeat.

**A:** Is Nina here?
**B:** Yes. She's over there.
**A:** Where? What does she have on?
**B:** She has on a red shirt and black pants.
**A:** OK. Thanks.

**B** Practice the conversation.

## 3 GRAMMAR: Adjective + noun

He has on a **white shirt.**
She has on a **red shirt** and **black pants.**

**Rob**

**Tina**

**Ling**

**Ed**

Complete the sentences.

**1.** Rob has on _gray pants and a white shirt_____.

**2.** Tina has on _____.

**3.** Ling has on _____.

**4.** Ed has on _____.

### Show what you know!

**1. WRITE ABOUT IT.** Look at a classmate. What clothing does your classmate have on?

My classmate has on _____ and _____.

**2. TELL THE CLASS.** Read your sentence to the class. Ask: *Who is it?*

I can describe clothing. ☐                    I need more practice. ☐

## Lesson 4 — Return Clothing to a Store

# What's the problem?

## 1 VOCABULARY: Problems with clothing

**A** ► Listen and point. Listen and repeat.

It's too small.

It's too big.

**B** ► Listen. Circle the problem.

1. too small      too big
2. too small      too big
3. too small      too big
4. too small      too big

## 2 CONVERSATION

**A** ► Listen. Listen and repeat.

**A:** I need to return this jacket and these shoes.
**B:** What's the problem?
**A:** The jacket is too big. The shoes are too small.
Here's my receipt.

**B** Circle *Yes* or *No*.

1. The man is buying a jacket and shoes.     Yes    No
2. The jacket is too small.     Yes    No
3. The shoes are too small.     Yes    No
4. He has a receipt.     Yes    No

**C** Practice the conversation.

# Return Clothing to a Store

**D** **WORK TOGETHER.** Look at the pictures. Make new conversations.

**A:** I need to return this _____ and these _____.

**B:** What's the problem?

**A:** The _____ is too _____. The _____
are too _____. Here's my receipt.

| Conversation 1 | Conversation 2 |
| --- | --- |
|  |  |

## Show what you know!

**1. TALK ABOUT IT.** Talk about the pictures.

A: What's the problem?

B: The skirt is too _____.

**2. WRITE ABOUT IT.** Write sentences about the pictures.

The skirt is too small.

I can return clothing to a store. ■             I need more practice. ■

# Life Skills: Read Store Ads

## Are shoes on sale?

## 1 READING

**A** Read the store ad.

CLOTHING MART  **Sale April 22-29**  HOME | WOMEN | MEN | CHILDREN

regular price $40.00
on sale $35.00

regular price $39.00
on sale $25.50

all skirts
on sale

regular price $38.99
on sale $30.00

all sweaters
on sale

regular price $69.99
on sale $59.99

**B** Answer the questions.

1. When is the sale? _____
2. What is the regular price for shoes? _____
3. What is the sale price for shoes? _____
4. What is the sale price for shirts? _____
5. How much can you save on jeans? _____
6. How much can you save on jackets? _____

## 2 WRITING

**A** ▶ Listen. Write the information.

Dan's Clothing Store    HOME | SPORTS & LEISURE | BUSINESS | RECREATIONAL    🔍

*Sale February 16-18*

Regular price $35.99

ON SALE _____

Regular price $29.00

ON SALE _____

Regular price $15.50

ON SALE _____

Regular price $52.99

ON SALE _____

Regular price $40.99

ON SALE _____

Regular price $75.00

ON SALE _____

**B** Read the ad again. Circle *Yes* or *No*.

| | | |
|---|---|---|
| 1. The sale starts on February 18. | Yes | No |
| 2. Sweaters are $35.99 on sale. | Yes | No |
| 3. Pants are $15.99 on sale. | Yes | No |
| 4. T-shirts are $15.50 on sale. | Yes | No |
| 5. Socks and shoes are on sale now. | Yes | No |
| 6. Jackets are on sale on February 16. | Yes | No |

**C** GO ONLINE.

1. Find a sale on a clothing store website.

2. Write the information.

Clothing item: _____    Sale price: _____

I can read store ads. ☐                         I need more practice. ☐

## 1 LISTENING

**A** Look at each picture. What do you see?

**B** ▶ Listen to the story.

# Read and Write About Clothing at a Wedding

## 2 READING

**A** ▶ Read and listen.

This is Yun. She lives in the United States. She is getting married.
Her wedding is in August. She needs a new dress. She wants a white dress.
In her native country, people wear white clothes at funerals.
Many women wear a red and green dress at their wedding.
Yun's mother and grandmother want her to have a red and green dress.

**B** Circle *Yes* or *No*.

| | | |
|---|---|---|
| **1.** Yun lives in her native country. | Yes | No |
| **2.** Yun's wedding is in October. | Yes | No |
| **3.** Yun wants a white dress. | Yes | No |
| **4.** In Yun's native country, women wear white dresses at weddings. | Yes | No |
| **5.** Yun's grandmother wants Yun to wear a red and green dress. | Yes | No |

## 3 WRITING

**A** **MAKE CONNECTIONS.** Talk about clothes in your native country.

**1.** What color clothes do people wear at funerals?
**2.** What color dress does a woman wear at her wedding?

**B** Complete the sentences.

**1.** In my native country, a woman wears _____ at her wedding.
**2.** In the United States, a woman wears _____ at her wedding.
**3.** In my native country, people wear _____ at a funeral.

**C** **WORK TOGETHER.** Read your sentences.

I can read and write about clothing at a wedding. ☐          I need more practice. ☐

# Omar is at work.

## 1 READING

Omar is an assistant manager.
He works at a clothing store.
He helps a customer return clothes.

## 2 CONVERSATION AT WORK

**A** Complete the conversation. Write the correct words.

Omar:       Good afternoon.
            _____?

Customer:   I need to _____ these pants.

Omar:       OK. What's the _____?

Customer:   They are too big.

Omar:       Do you have your receipt?

Customer:   Yes. _____.

Omar:       Thank you.

| Can I help you | Here you go |
| buy | return |
| problem | question |

| Here you go | I don't have it |

**B** Practice the conversation.

**C** Role-play the conversation with new information.

I can help a customer return clothes. ■            I need more practice. ■

# VOCABULARY REVIEW

**A** ► **LISTEN.** Listen and repeat.

| | | | | |
|---|---|---|---|---|
| beige | black | blue | brown | dress |
| gray | green | jacket | jeans | orange |
| pants | pink | purple | red | shirt |
| shoes | skirt | sneakers | socks | sweater |
| T-shirt | white | yellow | | |

**B** Write the words in the lists.

Colors

_____ _____ _____ _____ _____ _____

_____ _____ _____ _____ _____ _____

Clothing

_____ _____ _____ _____ _____ _____

_____ _____ _____ _____

**C** **WORK TOGETHER.** Look at the picture. What do you see? Write the colors and the clothes.

1. _____  2. _____  3. _____

4. _____  5. _____  6. _____

7. _____  8. _____

**D** Complete the sentences.

1. The green _____ is _____.

2. The red _____ is _____.

3. The blue _____ are _____.

4. The red _____ are _____.

# GRAMMAR REVIEW

**A** Complete the sentences. Write *this* or *these*.

1. Do you have _____these_____ shoes in size 7?
2. Do you have _____ jacket in medium?
3. _____ skirt is too big.
4. _____ shoes are too small.
5. I need to return _____ shirt and _____ pants.

**B** Complete the sentences. Write *that* or *those*.

1. _____Those_____ shirts are on sale.
2. What is the sale price for _____ jacket?
3. Do you like _____ dress?
4. Is _____ T-shirt on sale?
5. Are _____ sweaters on sale?

**C** Complete the sentences.

Jane        Vic        Tara        Ken        Amy

1. Jane has on _a white shirt and a gray skirt_____.
2. Vic has on _____.
3. Tara has on _____.
4. Ken has on _____.
5. Amy has on _____.

**ROLE-PLAY.**

**Student A**
You are a sales assistant.
You work in a clothing store.
Look at the picture.
Help Student B shop for clothing.

**Student B**
You are a customer.
You need clothing. You go shopping.
Look at the picture.
Ask for help in the store.

**A:** Can I help you?

**B:** Do you have _____?

**A:** No. I'm sorry. We don't. But we have _____.

**B:** Do you have _____ in _____?

**A:** Yes, here you are.

**Switch roles.**

**B:** Can I help you?

**A:** Do you have _____?

**B:** No. I'm sorry. We don't. But we have _____.

**A:** Do you have _____ in _____?

**B:** Yes, here you are.

GOOD LIFE CLOTHING

# SALE JUNE 5–19

Regular price: $45.00
*On sale: $29.00*

Regular price: $60.00
*On sale: $40.00*

Regular price: $30.00
*On sale: $25.00*

Regular price: $55.00
*On sale: $47.00*

Regular price: $69.00
*On sale: $45.50*

Regular price: $120.99
*On sale: $104.99*

**Read the store ad. Answer the questions.**

**1.** When does the sale start? _____

**2.** What is the sale price for sneakers? _____

**3.** How much do you save on sneakers? _____

**4.** What is the regular price for skirts? _____

**5.** What is the sale price for jeans? _____

**6.** What is the regular price for jackets? _____

**7.** How much do you save on jackets? _____

**8.** Are sweaters on sale? _____

**9.** When does the sale end? _____

**2** **WRITE ABOUT YOURSELF**

**Answer the question.**

Which clothing in the ad do you like?

_I like the red jacket._ _____

_____

**Unit Review:** Go back to page 141. Which unit goals can you check off?

# 9 Our Busy Lives

**PREVIEW**

Look at the picture. Who do you see?
What is she doing?

## UNIT GOALS

- [ ] Talk about what you do for fun
- [ ] Talk about what you are doing
- [ ] Ask about ongoing activities
- [ ] Talk about ongoing activities at work
- [ ] Read and write about weekend schedules
- [ ] **Life skills:** Leave a voicemail
- [ ] **English at work:** Take a personal call

# Talk About What You Do for Fun

## What do you do in your free time?

### 1 VOCABULARY: Free-time activities

**A** Look at the pictures. What do you see?

▶ Listen and point. Listen and repeat.

**B** ▶ Listen and read. Listen and repeat.

| | | |
|---|---|---|
| **1.** go online | **2.** play the guitar | **3.** listen to music |
| **4.** play soccer | **5.** exercise | **6.** watch TV |
| **7.** visit friends | **8.** go to the movies | **9.** play video games |

**C** **MAKE CONNECTIONS.** What do you do in your free time? Tell your partner.

*I play soccer. I go online.*

# Talk About What You Do for Fun

**D** ▶ Listen and point. Listen and repeat.

| February | | | | | | |
|---|---|---|---|---|---|---|
| Sunday | Monday | Tuesday | Wednesday | Thursday | Friday | Saturday |
| 1 | 2 | 3 | 4 | 5 | 6 | (7) |
| 8 | 9 | 10 | 11 | 12 | 13 | (14) |
| 15 | 16 | 17 | 18 | 19 | 20 | (21) |
| 22 | 23 | 24 | 25 | 26 | 27 | (28) |

- every Saturday
- once a week

| February | | | | | | |
|---|---|---|---|---|---|---|
| Sunday | Monday | Tuesday | Wednesday | Thursday | Friday | Saturday |
| 1 | (2) | 3 | (4) | 5 | 6 | 7 |
| 8 | (9) | 10 | (11) | 12 | 13 | 14 |
| 15 | (16) | 17 | (18) | 19 | 20 | 21 |
| 22 | (23) | 24 | (25) | 26 | 27 | 28 |

- every Monday and Wednesday
- twice a week

| February | | | | | | |
|---|---|---|---|---|---|---|
| Sunday | Monday | Tuesday | Wednesday | Thursday | Friday | Saturday |
| 1 | (2) | 3 | (4) | 5 | (6) | 7 |
| 8 | (9) | 10 | (11) | 12 | (13) | 14 |
| 15 | (16) | 17 | (18) | 19 | (20) | 21 |
| 22 | (23) | 24 | (25) | 26 | (27) | 28 |

- every Monday, Wednesday, and Friday
- three times a week

## 2 CONVERSATION

**A** ▶ Listen. Listen and repeat.

**A:** What do you do in your free time?
**B:** I listen to music. What do you do?
**A:** I play soccer.
**B:** How often?
**A:** Once a week.

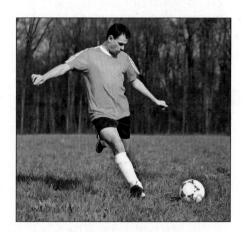

**B** Practice the conversation.

## Show what you know!

**1. WRITE ABOUT IT.** What do you do in your free time? Complete the chart.

| Activity | How Often? |
|---|---|
| | |

**2. TALK ABOUT IT.** Make new conversations.

A: What do you do in your free time?
B: I _____. What do you do?
A: I _____.
B: How often?
A: _____.

I can talk about what I do for fun. ■                    I need more practice. ☐

## Talk About What You Are Doing

# I'm watching a movie.

## 1 CONVERSATION

**A** ▶ Listen. Listen and repeat.

**A:** Hello?

**B:** Hi, Sara. It's Bill. What are you doing?

**A:** I'm watching a movie. Can I call you later?

**B:** No problem. Bye.

**A:** Goodbye.

Sara     Bill

**B** Practice the conversation.

## 2 GRAMMAR: Present continuous

| | |
|---|---|
| I **am** watch**ing** a movie. | I**'m** watch**ing** a movie. |
| You **are** watch**ing** a movie. | You**'re** watch**ing** a movie. |
| He **is** watch**ing** a movie. | He**'s** watch**ing** a movie. |
| She **is** watch**ing** a movie. | She**'s** watch**ing** a movie. |
| We **are** watch**ing** a movie. | We**'re** watch**ing** a movie. |
| They **are** watch**ing** a movie. | They**'re** watch**ing** a movie. |

**A** Complete the sentences.

**1.** I am _____watching_____ TV.
   watch

**2.** She is _____ the guitar.
   play

**3.** We are _____ to music.
   listen

**4.** They are _____ online.
   go

**5.** You are _____ video games.
   play

**6.** He is _____ friends.
   visit

**B** Write the answers.

1. **A:** What are you doing?

   **B:** (I / listen to music) *I'm listening to music.*

2. **A:** What is Mrs. White doing?

   **B:** (she / go online) _____

3. **A:** What are you doing?

   **B:** (we / visit friends) _____

4. **A:** What's Rob doing?

   **B:** (he / watch a movie) _____

5. **A:** What are Amy and David doing?

   **B:** (they / play video games) _____

**C** ▶ Listen and check your answers. Listen and repeat.

## Show what you know!

**1. WRITE ABOUT IT.** Look at the pictures. What are they doing?

**1.** He's *exercising* _____.

**2.** She's _____.

**3.** He's _____.

**4.** They're _____.

**2. TALK ABOUT IT.** What are they doing?

*He's exercising.*

| I can talk about what I am doing. ■ | I need more practice. ■ |
|---|---|

# Ask About Ongoing Activities

## Is he doing the laundry?

## 1 VOCABULARY: Activities at home

**A** Look at the pictures. What do you see?

▶ Listen and point. Listen and repeat.

**B** ▶ Listen and read. Listen and repeat.

| | | |
|---|---|---|
| **1.** walk the dog | **2.** pay bills | **3.** talk on the phone |
| **4.** do homework | **5.** wash the car | **6.** feed the cat |

**C** MAKE CONNECTIONS. What do you do at home?

**D** WORK TOGETHER. Tell your classmate what you do at home.

## 2 CONVERSATION

**A** ▶ Listen. Listen and repeat.

A: Hello?
B: Hi, Jin. How's everything going?
A: Great.
B: Is Alex doing the laundry?
A: Yes, he is.
B: Is Tina washing the car?
A: No, she's not. She's talking on the phone!

# Ask About Ongoing Activities

**B** Practice the conversation.

**C** **WORK TOGETHER.** Make new conversations.

**A:** Hello?
**B:** Hi, Jin. How's everything going?
**A:** Great.
**B:** Is Alex _____?
**A:** Yes, he is.
**B:** Is Tina _____?
**A:** No, she's not. She's _____!

## 3 GRAMMAR: Present continuous: *Yes / No* questions and answers

| Questions | Answers |
|---|---|
| **Are** you do**ing** homework? | Yes, **I am**. / No, **I'm not**. |
| **Is** Alex do**ing** homework? | Yes, **he is**. / No, **he's not**. |
| **Is** Tina do**ing** homework? | Yes, **she is**. / No, **she's not**. |
| **Are** the kids do**ing** homework? | Yes, **they are**. / No, **they're not**. |

Write questions.

1. (he / make dinner) *Is he making dinner?* _____
2. (they / play soccer) _____
3. (you / wash the car) _____
4. (Ester / do homework) _____
5. (you / talk on the phone) _____

## Show what you know!

**1. WRITE ABOUT IT.** Write three questions about the pictures on page 164.

*Is he* _____?

**2. TELL THE CLASS.** Ask your questions.

*Is he walking the dog?*

I can ask about ongoing activities. ☐          I need more practice. ☐

# She's not helping a customer.

## 1 VOCABULARY: Workplace activities

**A** Look at the pictures. What do you see?

▶ Listen and point. Listen and repeat.

**B** ▶ Listen and read. Listen and repeat.

| | | |
|---|---|---|
| **1.** work on the computer | **2.** help a customer | **3.** take a break |
| **4.** take orders | **5.** count money | **6.** look for something |
| **7.** answer the phone | **8.** drive a truck | **9.** fix cars |

**C** **WORK TOGETHER.** Point to a picture in Exercise A. Say the activity.

## 2 GRAMMAR: Present continuous negative

I'm **not** help**ing** a customer.
He**'s not** help**ing** a customer.
She**'s not** help**ing** a customer.
We**'re not** help**ing** a customer.
They**'re not** help**ing** a customer.

**A** Look at the pictures. Write sentences.

**1.** (she / drive a truck) _She's driving a truck._
**2.** (she / help a customer) _She's not helping a customer._

**3.** (he / count money) _____
**4.** (he / answer the phone) _____

**5.** (they / take a break) _____
**6.** (they / take orders) _____

**7.** (she / answer the phone) _____
**8.** (she / fix cars) _____

**B** ▶ Listen and check your answers. Listen and repeat.

## Show what you know!

**1. TALK ABOUT IT.** Point to a picture on page 166. Make two statements.

She's _____.
She's not _____.

**2. WRITE ABOUT IT.** Write your statements.

She's looking for something.
She's not answering the phone.

I can talk about ongoing activities at work. ☐          I need more practice. ☐

# 5

## Life Skills: Leave a Voicemail

# I'm not coming to work today.

## 1 VOCABULARY

▶ Listen and read. Listen and repeat.

**I'm late for work.**

**I'm sick.**

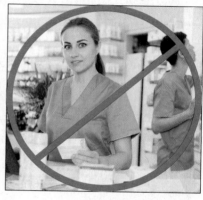

**I can't come to work today.**

## 2 READING

**A** ▶ Listen and read.

```
●●●○○ 🔋        7:28 AM          33% 🔋
    ‹        Voicemail          +

Victor Mata
May 23 at 7:23 AM
▶ ●──────────────────────────

This is Dan Green. Please leave a message.


Transcript
"Hi, Dan. This is Victor Mata. I'm
sorry, but I'm not coming to work
today. I'm sick."
```

**B** Circle *Yes* or *No*.

1. The message is for Dan Green.      Yes   No
2. Victor is calling Dan.              Yes   No
3. Victor is coming to work today.     Yes   No

**C** ▶ Listen and read.

**D** Circle *Yes* or *No*.

1. The message is for Tanya Smith.      Yes      No
2. Tanya is calling Dan.      Yes      No
3. Tanya is coming to work today.      Yes      No

**E** **WORK TOGETHER.** **Make your own voicemail. Say your sentences.**

This is _____. I'm sorry, but _____.

**F** GO ONLINE.

1. Use your phone to call a classmate or your teacher.
2. Leave a voicemail message.

I can leave a voicemail. ■                                          I need more practice. ■

# Read and Write About Weekend Schedules

## This is Luis.

### 1 LISTENING

**A** Look at each picture. What do you see?

**B** ▶ Listen to the story.

## 2 READING

**A** ▶ Read and listen.

This is Luis. He lives in the United States. He has two children.
His children are busy on weekends. They talk to their friends. They play sports.
Luis and his wife eat alone on weekends. Their children are busy every Saturday and Sunday.
In Luis's native country, families are together on weekends.
They spend time together. They talk.

**B** Circle *Yes* or *No*.

| | | |
|---|---|---|
| **1.** Luis's children are busy every weekend. | Yes | No |
| **2.** Luis plays sports every weekend. | Yes | No |
| **3.** On weekends, his family eats together. | Yes | No |
| **4.** In Luis's native country, families are together on weekends. | Yes | No |
| **5.** Luis spends time with his children on weekends. | Yes | No |

## 3 WRITING

**A** **MAKE CONNECTIONS.** Talk about families in your native country.

1. Are children busy on weekends? What do they do?
2. When do families eat together?
3. When do families spend time together?

**B** Complete the sentences.

1. In my native country, children _____ on weekends.
2. Families _____.
3. In the United States, children _____ on weekends.
4. Families _____.

**C** **WORK TOGETHER.** Read your sentences.

I can read and write about weekend schedules. ■          I need more practice. ☐

# English at Work: Take a Personal Call

## Pam is at work.

Pam

Ken

Front Desk

## 1 READING

Pam is a clerk.
She works in a hotel.
A friend calls her when she is working.

## 2 CONVERSATION AT WORK

**A** Complete the conversation. Write the correct words.

**Ken:** Hi, Pam. It's Ken. _____?

**Pam:** I'm working right now.

_____?

**Ken:** Oh! Sorry to bother you.

_____ working tonight?

**Pam:** No, I'm not. I'm _____ at 5:00.
I can call you then.

**Ken:** OK, great. Bye!

| What are you doing | What do you do |
|---|---|
| Can I help you | Can I call you later |

| Are you | Is he |
|---|---|
| going home | go home |

**B** Practice the conversation.

**C** Role-play the conversation with new information.

| I can take a personal call. ■ | I need more practice. ■ |
|---|---|

# VOCABULARY REVIEW

**A** ▶ **LISTEN. Listen and repeat.**

| | | |
|---|---|---|
| do homework | drive a truck | exercise |
| feed the cat | go to the movies | help a customer |
| pay bills | play soccer | take orders |
| visit friends | wash the car | work on the computer |

**B** Complete the chart. Use words from Exercise A.

| Free-Time Activities | Workplace Activities | Activities at Home |
|---|---|---|
| | | |
| | | |
| | | |
| | | |

**A** Look at the pictures. Write sentences. Use contractions.

1. _She's playing the guitar._

2. _____

3. _____

4. _____

5. _____

6. _____

**B** Complete the conversations.

1. **A:** _Are you doing the laundry_ _____? (you / do the laundry)
   **B:** Yes, I am.

2. **A:** _____? (she / wash the car)
   **B:** No, she's not.

3. **A:** Are they paying bills?
   **B:** Yes, _____.

4. **A:** Is she listening to music?
   **B:** No, _____.

5. **A:** _____? (they / visit friends)
   **B:** Yes, _____.

**C** Write sentences.

1. (I / not drive a truck)     _I'm not driving a truck._
2. (We / not walk the dog)   _____
3. (They / not listen to music)  _____
4. (Ella / not play soccer)    _____

## ROLE-PLAY.

**Student A**
Look at this picture. Ask questions.

**A:** What is _____ doing?
**B:** _____ is _____.

Mario     Fang     Alice     Alex

**Student B**
Answer Student A's questions.

**Student B**
Look at this picture. Ask questions.

**B:** What is _____ doing?
**A:** _____ is _____.

Mario     Fang     Alex     Alice

**Student A**
Answer Student B's questions.

## 1 LIFE SKILLS: Talk about your schedule

**A** ► Listen. Complete the schedule.

|  |  |
|---|---|
| Monday | work, school |
| Tuesday | _____ |
| Wednesday | work, _____ |
| Thursday | _____ |
| Friday | work, _____ |
| Saturday | soccer |
| Sunday | _____ |

7:27 PM    33%

**B** What do you do every week? Write your activities.

7:27 PM    33%

|  |  |
|---|---|
| Monday | _____ |
| Tuesday | _____ |
| Wednesday | _____ |
| Thursday | _____ |
| Friday | _____ |
| Saturday | _____ |
| Sunday | _____ |

**C** MAKE CONNECTIONS. Tell your classmates about your activities.

## 2 WRITE ABOUT YOURSELF

Complete the sentences.

1. My name is _____.
2. Once a week, I _____.
3. Every _____, I _____.
4. I _____ on weekends.

**Unit Review:** Go back to page 159. Which unit goals can you check off?

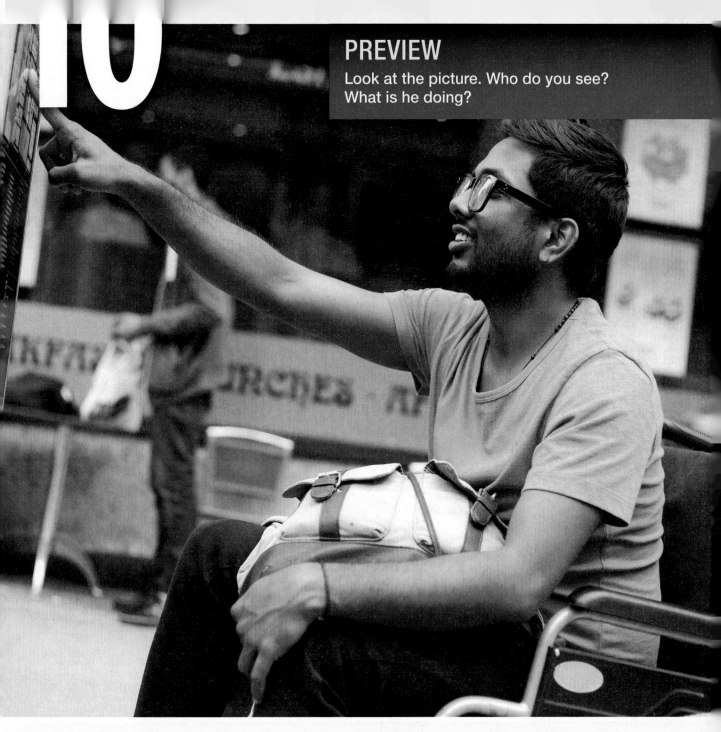

# 10

**PREVIEW**

Look at the picture. Who do you see?
What is he doing?

# UNIT GOALS

- ☐ Ask about places in the community
- ☐ Ask where places are
- ☐ Ask about transportation
- ☐ Ask for and give directions

- ☐ Read and write about transportation
- ☐ **Life skills:** Read traffic signs
- ☐ **English at work:** Give directions

# Is there a bank near here?

## 1 VOCABULARY: Places in the community

**A** Look at the pictures. What do you see?

▶ Listen and point. Listen and repeat.

**B** ▶ Listen and read. Listen and repeat.

| | | |
|---|---|---|
| **1.** a bank | **2.** a drugstore | **3.** a bus stop |
| **4.** a restaurant | **5.** an ATM | **6.** a hospital |
| **7.** a supermarket | **8.** a convenience store | **9.** a parking lot |

**C** ▶ Listen and look at the map. Point to the streets.

## 2 CONVERSATION

**A** ▶ Listen. Listen and repeat.

**A:** Excuse me. Is there a bank near here?
**B:** Yes. There's a bank on the corner of First Street and Central Avenue.
**A:** Thank you.

**B** Practice the conversation.

### Show what you know!

**1. TALK ABOUT IT.** Look at the map. Make new conversations.

A: Excuse me. Is there _____ near here?
B: Yes. There's _____ on the corner of _____
   and _____.
A: Thank you.

**2. WRITE ABOUT IT.** Write sentences.

There's a supermarket on the corner of Third Street and Central Avenue.

I can ask about places in the community. ■          I need more practice. ■

# Where is City Hall?

## 1 VOCABULARY: Public places

**A** Look at the pictures. What do you see?

▶ Listen and point. Listen and repeat.

**B** ▶ Listen and read. Listen and repeat.

| | | |
|---|---|---|
| **1.** police station | **2.** fire station | **3.** post office |
| **4.** library | **5.** park | **6.** courthouse |
| **7.** City Hall | **8.** Department of Motor Vehicles (DMV) | **9.** school |

**C** **WORK TOGETHER.** Point to a place in Exercise A. Say the place.

# Ask Where Places Are

## 2 CONVERSATION

▶ Listen. Listen and repeat. Then practice the conversation.

**A:** Excuse me. Where is City Hall?
**B:** It's between the police station and the DMV.
**A:** Between the police station and the DMV?
**B:** Yes. And it's across from the park.

## 3 GRAMMAR: *Between, across from*

| | |
|---|---|
| City Hall is **between** the police station and the DMV. | It's **across from** the park. |
| The post office is **between** the park and the library. | It's **across from** the DMV. |

**Look at the map. Complete the sentences.**

1. The DMV is between _the hospital and City Hall_____.
2. The hospital is across from _____.
3. The park is between _____.
4. The fire station is across from _____.

---

### Show what you know!

**1. TALK ABOUT IT.** Talk about places in your community.

A: Where is _____?
B: It's _____.

**2. WRITE ABOUT IT.** Write about places in your community.

The post office is across from the hospital.

---

| I can ask where places are. ■ | I need more practice. ■ |
|---|---|

## Ask About Transportation

# How do you get to work?

## 1 VOCABULARY: Getting to work

**A** Look at the pictures. What do you see?

▶ Listen and point. Listen and repeat.

**B** ▶ Listen and read. Listen and repeat.

| | | |
|---|---|---|
| **1.** walk | **2.** drive | **3.** carpool |
| **4.** ride a bike | **5.** take the bus | **6.** take the train |
| **7.** take the subway | **8.** take a taxi | **9.** take a ferry |

**C** MAKE CONNECTIONS. How do you get to work? Tell a partner.

*I walk. I take the bus.*

## 2 CONVERSATION

**A** ▶ Listen. Listen and repeat.

**A:** Hi, Ben. Where are you going?
**B:** I'm going to work.
**A:** Oh. How do you get to work?
**B:** I take the bus.

**B** Practice the conversation.

**C** ▶ Listen and read.

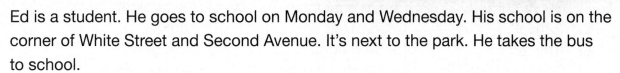

Ed is a student. He goes to school on Monday and Wednesday. His school is on the corner of White Street and Second Avenue. It's next to the park. He takes the bus to school.

**D** Circle *Yes* or *No*.

| | | | |
|---|---|---|---|
| **1.** Ed is a student. | | Yes | No |
| **2.** Ed goes to school on Monday. | | Yes | No |
| **3.** He takes the subway to school. | | Yes | No |
| **4.** His school is across from the park. | | Yes | No |

---

### Show what you know!

**1. WRITE ABOUT IT.** Ask your partner. Write your partner's information.

A: How do you get to _____?
B: I _____.

| Place | Type of Transportation |
|---|---|
| school | |
| supermarket | |
| work | |

**2. TELL THE CLASS.** Talk about your partner.

Manny takes a bus to school. He rides a bike to work.

---

I can ask about transportation. ■                    I need more practice. ■

# Ask for and Give Directions

# Where is the train station?

## 1 VOCABULARY: Directions

**A** ▶ Listen and point. Listen and repeat.

**Turn left.**　　　**Go straight.**　　　**Turn right.**　　　**Go two blocks.**

**B** ▶ Listen. Check (✓) the directions you hear.

| | | |
|---|---|---|
| **1.** ☐ Go straight. <br> ☐ Turn left. <br> ☐ Turn right. <br> ☐ Go two blocks. | **2.** ☐ Go straight. <br> ☐ Turn left. <br> ☐ Turn right. <br> ☐ Go two blocks. | **3.** ☐ Go straight. <br> ☐ Turn left. <br> ☐ Turn right. <br> ☐ Go two blocks. |
| **4.** ☐ Go straight. <br> ☐ Turn left. <br> ☐ Turn right. <br> ☐ Go two blocks. | **5.** ☐ Go straight. <br> ☐ Turn left. <br> ☐ Turn right. <br> ☐ Go two blocks. | **6.** ☐ Go straight. <br> ☐ Turn left. <br> ☐ Turn right. <br> ☐ Go two blocks. |

**C** ▶ Listen for the directions. Write each place on the map.

| bank | hospital | drugstore | post office | school |
|---|---|---|---|---|

**You Are Here**

# Ask for and Give Directions

## 2 CONVERSATION

**A** ▶ Listen. Listen and repeat.

**A:** Excuse me. Where is the train station?

**B:** It's on Park Street. Go straight for one block. Then turn left on Park Street.

**A:** Thanks a lot!

**B** Practice the conversation.

**C** **WORK TOGETHER.** Look at the maps. Make new conversations.

**A:** Excuse me. Where is the _____?

**B:** It's on _____. Go straight for _____.
Then turn _____.

**A:** Thanks a lot!

**Conversation 1**

**Conversation 2**

## Show what you know!

**1. TALK ABOUT IT.** Ask for and give directions. Use the map on page 184.

A: Excuse me. Where is _____?
B: It's _____. Go _____. Then _____.

**2. WRITE ABOUT IT.** Write about the places.

The post office is on White Street. It's across from City Hall.

| I can ask for and give directions. ▪ | I need more practice. ▫ |

# Lesson 5

## No parking.

### 1 VOCABULARY

**A** ▶ Listen and point. Listen and repeat.

**1**

stop

**2**

no left turn

**3**

walk     don't walk

**4**

do not enter

**5**

no parking

**6**

no U-turn

**7**

one-way street

**8**

speed limit 25 miles per hour

**9**

crosswalk

**B** MAKE CONNECTIONS. What signs do you see when you come to class?

**C** ▶ Listen. Write *1, 2, 3, 4, 5, 6* in the order you hear.

____

____

____

____

____

____

**D** **WORK TOGETHER.** Compare your answers.

## 2 READING

**A** ▶ Listen. Circle the correct sign.

1.

2.

3.

4.       

**B** GO ONLINE.

1. Find more traffic signs online.
2. Draw one new sign.
3. Talk about the sign. What does it mean?

I can read traffic signs. ■          I need more practice. ■

# Read and Write About Transportation

## This is Mohammed.

**1** LISTENING

Ⓐ Look at each picture. What do you see?

Ⓑ ▶ Listen to the story.

## 2 READING

**A** ▶ Read and listen.

> This is Mohammed.
>
> In Mohammed's native country, he takes the bus to get to work.
>
> He takes the subway to get to English class.
>
> He takes a taxi to go shopping.
>
> Mohammed lives in the United States. He has a car.
>
> In the United States, Mohammed drives to work. He drives to English class. He drives to go shopping.

**B** Circle *Yes* or *No*.

| | | |
|---|---|---|
| **1.** In his native country, Mohammed takes the bus to get to work. | Yes | No |
| **2.** In his native country, he takes a taxi to get to English class. | Yes | No |
| **3.** In the United States, Mohammed drives to work. | Yes | No |
| **4.** In the United States, Mohammed takes the bus to go shopping. | Yes | No |
| **5.** Mohammed has a car in the United States. | Yes | No |

## 3 WRITING

**A** MAKE CONNECTIONS. Talk about how people in your native country get around.

**1.** Do people take the bus?

**2.** Do people take the subway?

**3.** Do people take a taxi?

**4.** Do people have cars? Do they drive to work?

**B** Complete the sentences.

**1.** In my native country, some people _____ to work.

**2.** In the United States, some people _____ to work.

**C** WORK TOGETHER. Read your sentences.

---

I can read and write about transportation. ■      I need more practice. ■

# English at Work: Give Directions

## Ali is at work.

## 1 READING

Ali is a security guard.
He works at a bank.
He gives directions to a customer.

## 2 CONVERSATION AT WORK

**A** Complete the conversation. Write the correct words.

**Customer:** Excuse me. _____ library?

**Ali:** Go two blocks and turn left. It's _____ the fire station.

**Customer:** I'm sorry. Can you repeat that?

**Ali:** _____. Go two blocks and turn left on Park Street.

**Customer:** Go two blocks and turn left. I understand. Thank you!

**Ali:** _____!

| Where is the | There is the |
| --- | --- |

| between | across from |
| --- | --- |

| No problem | No, I'm sorry |
| --- | --- |

| You're welcome | Excuse me |
| --- | --- |

**B** Practice the conversation.

**C** Role-play the conversation with new information.

| I can give directions. ■ | I need more practice. ■ |
| --- | --- |

**A** ▶ **LISTEN.** Listen and repeat.

ATM
library

bank
police station

drugstore
supermarket

**B** Complete the sentences. Use words from Exercise A.

1. **A:** I need money.
   **B:** Go to the _____.

2. **A:** I need food.
   **B:** Go to the _____.

3. **A:** I need help.
   **B:** Go to the _____.

4. **A:** I need a credit card.
   **B:** Go to the _____.

5. **A:** I need soap.
   **B:** Go to the _____.

6. **A:** I need a book.
   **B:** Go to the _____.

**C** Write the type of transportation.

1. _____

2. _____

3. _____

4. _____

5. _____

6. _____

7. _____

8. _____

# GRAMMAR REVIEW

**A** Write *between*, *across from*, or *on*.

1. The parking lot is ___across from___ the hospital.

2. City Hall is _____ the post office and the DMV.

3. The hospital is _____ Park Street.

4. The bank is _____ the corner of Second Avenue and Park Street.

5. The courthouse is _____ First Avenue.

*(Map showing:)*
supermarket, police station, First Avenue, courthouse, restaurant, post office, library, hospital, parking lot, City Hall, DMV, Second Avenue, bus stop, bank, school, park, drugstore, Park Street, Main Street, Third Avenue

**B** Look at the map. Write questions with *Where*.

1. **A:** _Where is the courthouse?_____
   **B:** It's between the police station and the restaurant.

2. **A:** _____
   **B:** It's on the corner of First Avenue and Park Street.

3. **A:** _____
   **B:** It's between the bank and the school.

4. **A:** _____
   **B:** It's across from the parking lot.

5. **A:** _____
   **B:** It's across from the bank.

6. **A:** _____
   **B:** It's on the corner of Second Avenue and Main Street. It's across from the park.

**C** Complete the conversations. Use *go* or *turn*.

1. **A:** Excuse me. Where is the bus stop?
   **B:** _____Go_____ straight for one block. Then _____ right.

2. **A:** Where is the library?
   **B:** _____ left. Then _____ three blocks.

3. **A:** Where is City Hall?
   **B:** _____ straight for one block. Then _____ left.
   _____ two blocks. It's on Grand Street.

## ROLE-PLAY.

**Student A**
Ask Student B for directions to:

the hospital
the drugstore
the parking lot

**Student B**
Look at the map.
Listen to Student A.
Give directions

**A:** Excuse me. Where is the _____?

**B:** It's _____. Go _____. Then turn _____.

**Student B**
Ask Student A for directions to:

the bank
the gas station
the computer store

**Student A**
Look at the map.
Listen to Student B.
Give directions

**B:** Excuse me. Where is the _____?

**A:** It's _____. Go _____. Then turn _____.

## 1 LIFE SKILLS: Read traffic signs

Look at the pictures. What signs do you see? Write the signs.

1. _____

2. _____

3. _____

4. _____

5. _____

6. _____

## 2 WRITE ABOUT YOURSELF

Complete the sentences.

**1.** How do you get to work?

_____.

**2.** How do you get to school?

_____.

**3.** What signs do you see every day?

_____.

**4.** What places in the community do you go to every day?

_____.

**Unit Review:** Go back to page 177. Which unit goals can you check off?

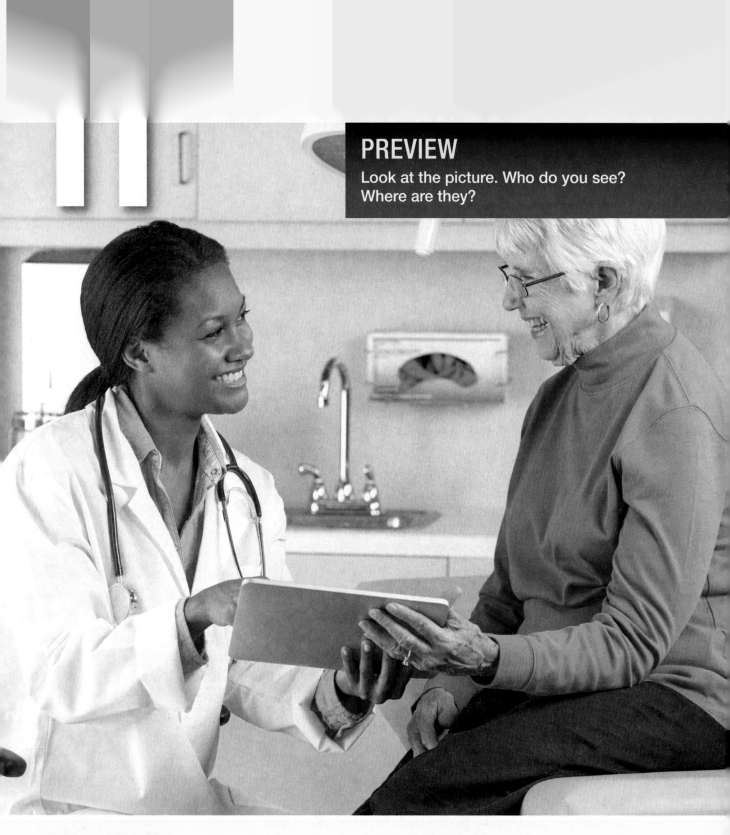

## PREVIEW

Look at the picture. Who do you see?
Where are they?

# UNIT GOALS

- ☐ Make an appointment
- ☐ Listen to a doctor
- ☐ Offer suggestions
- ☐ Call 911 for emergencies
- ☐ Read and write about a doctor's appointment
- ☐ **Life skills:** Read a medicine label
- ☐ **English at work:** Help someone make an appointment

# Make an Appointment

# My back hurts.

## 1 VOCABULARY: The body

**A** Look at the pictures. What do you see?

▶ Listen and point. Listen and repeat.

**B** ▶ Listen and read. Listen and repeat.

| | | | |
|---|---|---|---|
| **1.** head | **2.** mouth | **3.** ear | **4.** eye |
| **5.** nose | **6.** neck | **7.** chest | **8.** stomach |
| **9.** hand | **10.** shoulder | **11.** back | **12.** arm |
| **13.** knee | **14.** leg | **15.** foot / feet | |

**C** **WORK TOGETHER.** Point to the pictures. Your partner says the word.

# Make an Appointment

Tom

## 2 CONVERSATION

**A** ▶ **Listen. Listen and repeat.**

**A:** Hello. Westside Health Clinic.

**B:** This is Tom Perez. I'd like to make an appointment.

**A:** What's the problem?

**B:** My back hurts.

**A:** Can you come in at 4:00?

**B:** Yes, I can.

**B** Practice the conversation.

**C** **WORK TOGETHER.** Make new conversations.

**A:** Hello. Westside Health Clinic.

**B:** This is _____. I'd like to make an appointment.

**A:** What's the problem?

**B:** My _____ hurts.

**A:** Can you come in at 4:00?

**B:** Yes, I can.

---

## Show what you know!

**1. TALK ABOUT IT.** Role-play a conversation.

Student A has a problem. Call the clinic.
Student B works at the clinic. Answer the phone. Talk to Student A.

**2. WRITE ABOUT IT.** Perform your conversations for the class.
Write a sentence about each problem you hear.

*Tom's back hurts.*

---

I can make an appointment. ■                I need more practice. ■

## 1 VOCABULARY: Medical instructions

**A** Look at the pictures. What do you see?

▶ Listen and point. Listen and repeat.

**B** ▶ Listen and read. Listen and repeat.

1. Take off your jacket.
4. Breathe in.
7. Open your mouth.

2. Step on the scale.
5. Breathe out.
8. Roll up your sleeves.

3. Sit on the table.
6. Look straight ahead.
9. Lie down.

**C** **WORK TOGETHER.** Tell your partner what to do. Follow your partner's instructions.

# Listen to a Doctor

## 2 CONVERSATION

**A** ▶ **Listen. Listen and repeat.**

**A:** Hello. I'm Dr. Medina. Why are you here today?
**B:** I'm here for a checkup.
**A:** OK. Sit on the table. Look straight ahead.

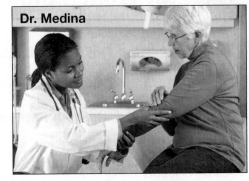

Dr. Medina

**B** **Practice the conversation.**

**C** ▶ **Listen and read.**

Isabel gets a checkup every year. She goes to the health clinic.
Her appointment is on Monday. Her doctor says, "You are healthy."

**D** **Circle *Yes* or *No*.**

| | | |
|---|---|---|
| 1. Isabel gets a checkup every year. | Yes | No |
| 2. Isabel has an appointment on Tuesday. | Yes | No |
| 3. Her appointment is at the school. | Yes | No |
| 4. Isabel is sick. | Yes | No |

---

## Show what you know!

**1. WRITE ABOUT IT.** What do you do at the doctor's office?

*I step on the scale.*

**2. TALK ABOUT IT.** Tell your partner.

---

I can listen to a doctor. ■                    I need more practice. ■

## Offer Suggestions

# What's the matter?

## 1 VOCABULARY: Health problems

(A) Look at the pictures. What do you see?

▶ Listen and point. Listen and repeat.

(B) ▶ Listen and read. Listen and repeat.

| | | |
|---|---|---|
| **1.** a headache | **2.** a backache | **3.** a stomachache |
| **4.** a toothache | **5.** a cold | **6.** a cough |
| **7.** a fever | **8.** the flu | **9.** a sore throat |

(C) **WORK TOGETHER.** Point to a picture. Say the problem. Use *She has* ____ or *He has* ____.

# Offer Suggestions

## 2 CONVERSATION

**A** ▶ Listen. Listen and repeat.

**A:** What's the matter?

**B:** I have a cold.

**A:** You should drink a lot of liquids.

**B** Practice the conversation.

## 3 GRAMMAR: *Should*

 You **should drink** a lot of liquids.

 You **should get** a lot of rest.

 You **should take** aspirin.

 You **should stay** home from work.

Write sentences. Use *should*.

1. you / go to the doctor  *You should go to the doctor.*

2. he / get a checkup  _____

3. they / take a break  _____

4. I / do homework  _____

5. we / go online  _____

6. you / go to work  _____

### Show what you know!

**1. TALK ABOUT IT.** Make new conversations.

A: What's the matter?

B: I have a _____.

A: You should _____.

**2. WRITE ABOUT IT.** Write your suggestions.

You should drink tea.

I can offer suggestions. ☐                    I need more practice. ☐

## What's your emergency?

### 1 VOCABULARY: Emergencies

**A** Look at the pictures. What do you see?

▶ Listen and point. Listen and repeat.

**B** ▶ Listen and read. Listen and repeat.

1. My friend is having a heart attack.
2. There was a car accident.
3. There is a building on fire.
4. Someone robbed my house.

**C** **WORK TOGETHER.** Point to a picture. Say the emergency.

# Call 911 for Emergencies

## 2 CONVERSATION

**A** ▶ Listen. Listen and repeat.

**A:** 911. What's your emergency?
**B:** My friend is having a heart attack.
**A:** Where are you?
**B:** 1038 Park Avenue.
**A:** What's the cross street?
**B:** River Road.

River Road

Park Avenue          1038 Park Avenue

**B** Circle *Yes* or *No*.

| | | |
|---|---|---|
| 1. There is an emergency. | Yes | No |
| 2. Someone is having a heart attack. | Yes | No |
| 3. The emergency is on River Road. | Yes | No |
| 4. The cross street is Park Avenue. | Yes | No |

**C** Practice the conversation.

## Show what you know!

**1. TALK ABOUT IT.** Make new conversations.

A: 911. What's your emergency?
B: _____.
A: Where are you?
B: _____.
A: What's the cross street?
B: _____.

**2. TELL THE CLASS.** Perform one of your conversations.

I can call 911 for emergencies. ☐          I need more practice. ☐

## 1 VOCABULARY

**A** ▶ Listen and read. Listen and repeat.

cough syrup

aspirin

prescription medicine

teaspoon

tablets

capsules

pills

8:00 a.m.
12:00 p.m.
4:00 p.m.
8:00 p.m.

**every 4 hours**

8:00 a.m.
2:00 p.m.
8:00 p.m.

**every 6 hours**

8:00 a.m.
8:00 p.m.

**twice a day**

**B** ▶ Listen. Circle the correct words.

Conversation 1

**1.** The woman is taking ____.
   aspirin
   cough syrup

**2.** She should take ____.
   2 teaspoons every hour
   2 teaspoons every 4 hours

Conversation 2

**3.** The man is taking ____.
   prescription medicine
   cough syrup

**4.** The directions say take 1 capsule ____.
   twice a day with food
   every hour with food

## 2 READING

**A** Read the directions on the label.

**Aspirin**
for aches and pain relief
and to reduce fever

Directions:
Adults and children 12 years and over:
Take 2 tablets with water
every 4 hours.

If fever continues, see a doctor.

**B** Look at the label in Exercise A. Circle the correct words.

**1.** The medicine is for _____.

    coughs                                     pain and fever

**2.** Ben has a headache and a fever. He should _____.

    take aspirin                            take cough syrup

**3.** Ben is 25 years old. He should _____.

    take 2 tablets                         take 3 tablets

**4.** Ben should take the aspirin _____.

    every 2 hours                        every 4 hours

**5.** Ben has a fever for 5 days. He should _____.

    take more aspirin                    see a doctor

**C** GO ONLINE.

**1.** Search online for images of medicine labels.

**2.** Write the instructions.

Name of medicine: _____

Take _____ every _____.

Who should take the medicine? _____

I can read a medicine label. ◻                      I need more practice. ◻

# This is Teresa.

## 1 LISTENING

**A** Look at each picture. What do you see?

**B** ▶ Listen to the story.

## 2 READING

**A** ▶ Read and listen.

This is Teresa. She is 45 years old.
In Teresa's native country, people go to the doctor when they are sick.
Teresa lives in the United States. Her daughter wants her to get a checkup.
Her daughter says people should go to the doctor every year.
Teresa feels healthy. She does not want to get a checkup.

**B** Circle *Yes* or *No*.

| | | |
|---|---|---|
| **1.** Teresa is 40 years old. | Yes | No |
| **2.** In Teresa's native country, people go to the doctor when they are sick. | Yes | No |
| **3.** Teresa's daughter does not want her to get a checkup. | Yes | No |
| **4.** Teresa's daughter says she should get a checkup every year. | Yes | No |
| **5.** Teresa wants to go to the doctor. | Yes | No |

## 3 WRITING

**A** MAKE CONNECTIONS. Talk about doctor's appointments in your native country.

1. How often do people go to the doctor?
2. Do people get a checkup every year?

**B** Complete the sentences.

1. In my native country, people go to the doctor _____.
2. In the United States, people go to the doctor _____.

**C** WORK TOGETHER. Read your sentences.

---

I can read and write about a doctor's appointment. ■ I need more practice. ■

# Lila is at work.

Lila

Patient

## 1 READING

Lila is a nursing assistant.
She works in a clinic.
She helps a patient make an appointment.

## 2 CONVERSATION AT WORK

**A** Complete the conversation. Write the correct words.

**Lila:** Thank you for calling Sunshine Clinic. How can I help you?

**Patient:** Hello. _____.

| I'm here for a checkup | I'd like to make an appointment |

**Lila:** OK. _____?

**Patient:** My neck hurts. I want to see a doctor.

| Can you come in at 3:00 | What's the problem |

**Lila:** Of course! _____?

| Can you come in at 3:00 | What's the problem |

**Patient:** No, I can't. I can come in after 3:30.

**Lila:** OK. How about 4:00?

**Patient:** Perfect. Thank you.

**Lila:** See you then!

**B** Practice the conversation.

**C** Role-play the conversation with new information.

I can help someone make an appointment. ■          I need more practice. ■

# VOCABULARY REVIEW

**A** ▶ Listen. Listen and repeat.

| | | | | |
|---|---|---|---|---|
| arm | back | chest | ear | eye |
| foot / feet | hand | knee | leg | neck |
| nose | shoulder | stomach | | |

**B** **WORK TOGETHER.** Point to each part of the body. Say the name.

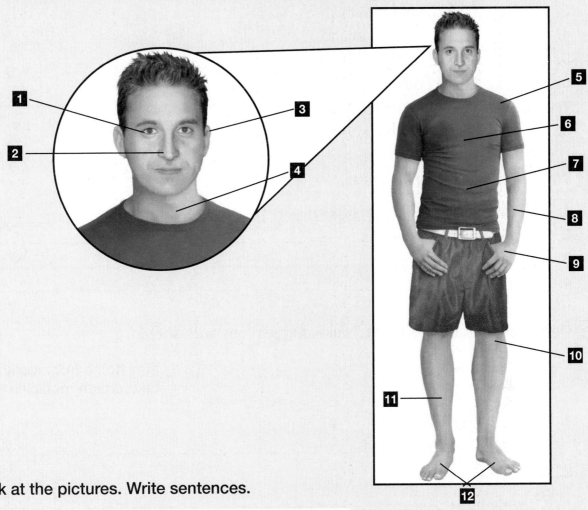

**C** Look at the pictures. Write sentences.

| | | |
|---|---|---|
| a cold | a headache | a backache |

1. _____

2. _____

3. _____

# GRAMMAR REVIEW

**A** Complete the sentences.

| | | | |
|---|---|---|---|
| breathe | lie | look | open |
| roll | sit | ~~step~~ | take off |

1. _____Step_____ on the scale.
2. _____ in.
3. _____ your mouth.
4. _____ straight ahead.
5. _____ up your sleeves.
6. _____ down.
7. _____ your jacket.
8. _____ on the table.

**B** Write sentences. Use *I'd like to*.

1. (talk to a doctor) _I'd like to talk to a doctor._
2. (make an appointment) _____
3. (talk to a nurse) _____
4. (see a doctor) _____

**C** Complete the conversations. Make suggestions with *should*.

| | |
|---|---|
| ~~drink liquids~~ | stay home from work |
| take aspirin | take cough medicine |

1. **A:** I have a sore throat.

   **B:** _You should drink liquids._

2. **A:** I have a headache.

   **B:** _____

3. **A:** I have a cough.

   **B:** _____

4. **A:** I have the flu.

   **B:** _____

**ROLE-PLAY.**

**Student A**
You don't feel well.
You have a headache and a cough.

**Student B**
You are Student A's friend.
Give suggestions.

**A:** What's the matter?

**B:** I have _____.

**A:** You should _____.

**Student B**
You don't feel well.
You have the flu and a stomachache.

**Student A**
You are Student B's friend.
Give suggestions.

**B:** What's the matter?

**A:** I have _____.

**B:** You should _____.

Read the label. Then complete the sentences and answer the questions.

**Cough Syrup**

*Take for coughs, not for fevers.*
*Directions:*
**Adults:** Take 2 teaspoons every 4–6 hours.

**Children 6–12 years:** Take 1 teaspoon every 4–6 hours.

Children under 6: See a doctor for instructions.

**1.** What medicine is it? _____

**2.** Adults should take _____ teaspoons.

**3.** Adults should take the medicine _____ hours.

**4.** A 12-year-old child should take _____.

**5.** A 12-year-old child should take the medicine _____ hours.

**6.** Your child is 5. What should you do?

_____

**2** **WRITE ABOUT YOURSELF**

Answer the questions.

**1.** What do you do for a sore throat? _____

**2.** What do you do for a headache? _____

**3.** What do you do for a cough? _____

**4.** What do you do for a cold? _____

**Unit Review:** Go back to page 195. Which unit goals can you check off?

# 12 What Do You Do?

## PREVIEW

Look at the picture. Who do you see?
What is she doing?

## UNIT GOALS

- ☐ Say your occupation
- ☐ Ask about someone's job
- ☐ Talk about job skills
- ☐ Apply for a job

- ☐ Read and write about a job interview
- ☐ **Life skills:** Read a job ad
- ☐ **English at work:** Apply for a new job

# I'm a teacher's assistant.

## 1 VOCABULARY: Jobs

**A** Look at the pictures. What do you see?

▶ Listen and point. Listen and repeat.

**B** ▶ Listen and read. Listen and repeat.

| | | |
|---|---|---|
| **1.** a mechanic | **2.** a nursing assistant | **3.** a painter |
| **4.** a construction worker | **5.** a teacher's assistant | **6.** a sales assistant |
| **7.** a dentist | **8.** a housekeeper | **9.** a bus driver |

**C** **WORK TOGETHER.** Point to a picture. Your partner says the job.

## 2 CONVERSATION

**A** ▶ Listen. Listen and repeat.

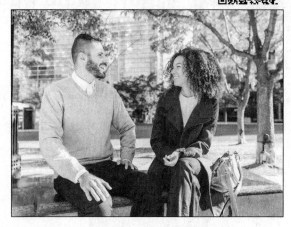

**A:** Let's get coffee.

**B:** I'm sorry. I can't. I have to go to work.

**A:** Oh. What do you do?

**B:** I'm a teacher's assistant.

**B** Practice the conversation.

**C** WORK TOGETHER.  Make new conversations. Use the jobs on page 214.

**A:** Let's get coffee.

**B:** I'm sorry. I can't. I have to go to work.

**A:** Oh. What do you do?

**B:** I'm a _____.

## Show what you know!

1. **TALK ABOUT IT.**  Ask classmates: *What do you do?*
   Write the information.

| Name | Job |
|------|-----|
| Omar | mechanic |
|  |  |
|  |  |
|  |  |
|  |  |

2. **WRITE ABOUT IT.**  Write sentences.

*Omar is a mechanic.*

| I can say my occupation. ■ | I need more practice. ■ |
|---|---|

# Ask About Someone's Job

## Where does he work?

## 1 VOCABULARY: More jobs

**A** Look at the pictures. What do you see?

▶ Listen and point. Listen and repeat.

**B** ▶ Listen and read. Listen and repeat.

| | | |
|---|---|---|
| **1.** a cashier | **2.** a doctor | **3.** a factory worker |
| **4.** a cook | **5.** a nurse | **6.** an office assistant |
| **7.** a security guard | **8.** a server | **9.** a custodian |

**C** **WORK TOGETHER.** Point to a picture. Say the job.

# Ask About Someone's Job

## 2 CONVERSATION

**A** ▶ Listen. Listen and repeat.

Bo

**A:** Who's that?

**B:** That's Bo. He's a nurse.

**A:** Where does he work?

**B:** He works at Valley Hospital.

**B** Practice the conversation.

## 3 GRAMMAR: *Where do, where does*

| | |
|---|---|
| **Where do** you work? | **Where does** he work? |
| **Where do** they work? | **Where does** she work? |

Complete the conversations. Write *do* or *does*.

**1. A:** Where _____ *does* _____ Gino work?
   **B:** He works at a café.

**2. A:** Where _____ you work?
   **B:** I work at a restaurant.

**3. A:** Where _____ Yuki work?
   **B:** She works at home.

**4. A:** Where _____ Ivan work?
   **B:** He works at a school.

**5. A:** Where _____ Hannah and Sasha work?
   **B:** They work at a hotel.

### Show what you know!

**1. TALK ABOUT IT.** Ask about your partner.

*What do you do?*
*Where do you work?*

**2. TELL THE CLASS.** Talk about your partner.

*Mina is a cook. She works in a restaurant.*

I can ask about someone's job. ■                    I need more practice. ■

# Talk About Job Skills

## What are your job skills?

### 1 VOCABULARY: Job skills

**A** Look at the pictures. What do you see?

▶ Listen and point. Listen and repeat.

**B** ▶ Listen and read. Listen and repeat.

| | | |
|---|---|---|
| **1.** speak two languages | **2.** use a cash register | **3.** help customers |
| **4.** use a computer | **5.** use office machines | **6.** build houses |
| **7.** fix something | **8.** operate machinery | **9.** take care of patients |

**C** **WORK TOGETHER.** Point to a picture. Say the job skill.

# Talk About Job Skills

## 2 CONVERSATION

**A** ▶ Listen. Listen and repeat.

**A:** What are your job skills?
**B:** I can use a computer.
And I can use a cash register.
**A:** What other skills do you have?
**B:** I can speak two languages.

**B** Practice the conversation.

**C** ▶ Listen and read.

Grace needs a new job. She has an interview on Wednesday. Grace has many skills. She can use a computer and a cash register. Grace can also speak two languages.

**D** Circle *Yes* or *No*.

| | | | |
|---|---|---|---|
| **1.** | Grace wants a new job. | Yes | No |
| **2.** | She has an interview on Monday. | Yes | No |
| **3.** | Grace can use a cash register. | Yes | No |
| **4.** | She can speak three languages. | Yes | No |

## Show what you know!

**1. WRITE ABOUT IT.** What are your job skills?

I can _____. And I can _____.

**2. TALK ABOUT IT.** Ask about your partner's job skills.

A: What are your job skills?
B: I can use a computer. And I can speak two languages.

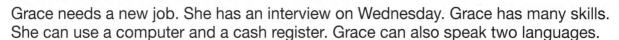

I can talk about job skills. ☐                    I need more practice. ☐

# Apply for a Job

## I'd like to apply for the office assistant job.

### 1 CONVERSATION

**A** ▶ **Listen. Listen and repeat.**

**A:** Hello. I'd like to apply for the office assistant job.

**B:** OK. Can you use a computer?

**A:** Yes, I can.

**B:** Please fill out the application.

**A:** Thank you.

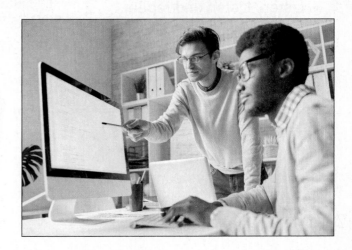

**B** Circle *Yes* or *No*.

| | | |
|---|---|---|
| **1.** The man wants a mechanic job. | Yes | No |
| **2.** The man can use a computer. | Yes | No |
| **3.** The man should fill out the application. | Yes | No |

**C** Practice the conversation.

**C** **WORK TOGETHER.** Read the job ads. Make new conversations.

**A:** Hello. I'd like to apply for the _____ job.

**B:** OK. Can you _____?

**A:** Yes, I can.

**B:** Please fill out the application.

**A:** Thank you.

**Conversation 1**

● ● ●

**Mechanic needed to fix cars**

**Conversation 2**

● ● ●

**Sales assistant needed to help customers**

**Conversation 3**

● ● ●

**Construction worker needed to build houses**

## 2 GRAMMAR: *Can*

| | |
|---|---|
| **Can** you **use** a computer? | **Yes**, I **can**.<br>**No**, I **can't**. |
| **Can** Mr. Vega **use** a computer? | **Yes**, he **can**.<br>**No**, he **can't**. |
| **Can** Nancy **use** a computer? | **Yes**, she **can**.<br>**No**, she **can't**. |
| **Can** Alex and Chris **use** a computer? | **Yes**, they **can**.<br>**No**, they **can't**. |

**A** Write the questions and answers.

1. **A:** <u>Can Miss Tang serve customers?</u> (can / Miss Tang / serve customers)
   **B:** Yes, <u>she can</u>.

2. **A:** _____ (can / Mr. Black / use a computer)
   **B:** No, _____.

3. **A:** _____ (can / you / build houses)
   **B:** Yes, _____.

4. **A:** _____ (can / Marina and Pedro / help customers)
   **B:** Yes, _____.

5. **A:** _____ (can / Ella / speak two languages)
   **B:** No, _____.

**B** ▶ Listen and check your answers. Listen and repeat.

### Show what you know!

1. **TALK ABOUT IT.** Ask: *Can you* _____? Check (✓) your partner's job skills.

   ☐ speak two languages      ☐ use office machines
   ☐ take care of patients     ☐ use a cash register
   ☐ use a computer            ☐ fix things

2. **WRITE ABOUT IT.** Write sentences about your partner.

   *Trina can use a cash register and a computer.*

| I can apply for a job. ■ | I need more practice. ■ |
|---|---|

# I can work with a team.

## 1 VOCABULARY

**A** Complete the sentences. Use words from the box.

| apply online | full-time | go in person | part-time | required | weekdays | weekends |

1. I work 15 hours a week. I work _____.
2. I work 40 hours a week. I work _____.
3. I work on Saturdays and Sundays. I work _____.
4. I work Monday to Friday. I work _____.
5. I have to go to the office for my interview. I have to _____.
6. I need to have experience for this job. Experience is _____.
7. I need to fill out an application on a website. I have to _____.

**B** ▶ Listen and read. Listen and repeat.

**I can work with a team.**

**I can work independently.**

**I can communicate well.**

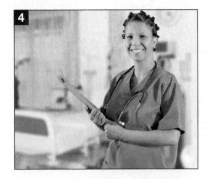
**I have a positive attitude.**

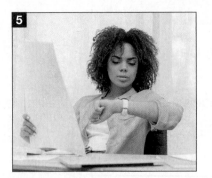
**I manage my time well.**

**I can work under pressure.**

## 2 READING

**A** MAKE CONNECTIONS. What skills do you have?

*I manage my time well.*

**B** Read the job ads.

**Help Wanted**
Sales Assistant
1 year experience required
Must work well under pressure
Full-time evenings and
 weekends
Apply online: BestStores.com

A

**Job Available**
Cashier
No experience required
Must communicate well and
 work with a team
Part-time 25 hours / week
Call Ella Lopez: 616-555-9543

B

**Driver Needed**
Full-time 35 hours / week
2 years experience required
Must work independently
Apply in person:
ABC Company
300 Plaza Avenue

C

**C** Match the sentences with the ads. Write *A, B,* or *C.*

**1.** This job is full-time evenings and weekends. _____

**2.** You need two years of experience. _____

**3.** You need to work with a team. _____

**4.** You need to apply in person. _____

**5.** This job is 35 hours a week. _____

**6.** You need to work well under pressure. _____

**7.** You need to work independently. _____

**8.** You need to apply online. _____

**D** GO ONLINE.

**1.** Find a job ad online.

**2.** Write the skills you need for the job.

| I can read a job ad. ■ | I need more practice. ■ |

# Read and Write About a Job Interview

## This is Monika.

**A** Look at each picture. What do you see?

**B** ▶ Listen to the story.

# Read and Write About a Job Interview

## 2 READING

**A** ▶ Read and listen.

> This is Monika. She lives in the United States.
> Monika has a job interview on Thursday at 9:00.
> Monika is ready for the interview. She practiced her interview skills in her English class.
> Monika gets to the interview. She is early. She says hello and smiles.
> She shakes hands with Mr. Cruz.
> Mr. Cruz asks about Monika's job skills. She answers his questions.

**B** Circle *Yes* or *No*.

1. Monika has a job interview on Tuesday.          Yes   No
2. She practiced her interview skills.             Yes   No
3. She gets to the interview early.                Yes   No
4. She hugs Mr. Cruz.                              Yes   No
5. She answers Mr. Cruz's questions.               Yes   No

## 3 WRITING

**A** **MAKE CONNECTIONS.** Talk about job interviews in your native country.

1. Do people arrive on time for job interviews?
2. Do people practice their interview skills?
3. Do people shake hands with the interviewer?

**B** Complete the sentences.

1. In my native country, people arrive _____ for job interviews.
2. They _____ with the interviewer.
3. In the United States, people arrive _____ for job interviews.
4. They _____ with the interviewer.

**C** **WORK TOGETHER.** Read your sentences.

I can read and write about a job interview. ■          I need more practice. ■

# English at Work: Apply for a New Job

## Van is at work.

Van              Manager

## 1 READING

Van is a mechanic.
He works at a car repair shop.
He wants to apply for a new job.

## 2 CONVERSATION AT WORK

**A** Complete the conversation. Write the correct words.

| | |
|---|---|
| **Van:** | Hello. _____ the job. |
| **Manager:** | OK. Do you have experience? |
| **Van:** | Yes, I do. I work at Tom's Cars now. |
| | I have five years of _____ . |
| **Manager:** | That's great! When _____? |
| **Van:** | I can start next week! |
| **Manager:** | OK. Please _____ . |
| **Van:** | Thank you! I can do it now. |

| | |
|---|---|
| I'd like to apply for | I want |
| experience | attitude |
| do you work | can you begin work |
| apply in person | fill out an application |

**B** Practice the conversation.

**C** Role-play the conversation with new information.

| I can apply for a new job. ■ | I need more practice. ■ |
|---|---|

## A ▶ Listen. Listen and repeat.

| | | | |
|---|---|---|---|
| build houses | cashier | communicate well | doctor |
| drive a truck | fix something | help customers | housekeeper |
| manage time well | mechanic | nurse | office assistant |
| sales assistant | server | speak two languages | take care of patients |
| teacher | teacher's assistant | use a computer | work with a team |

## B Complete the chart. Use words from Exercise A.

| Jobs | Skills |
|---|---|
| | |
| | |
| | |
| | |
| | |
| | |
| | |
| | |
| | |

## C Match the jobs and the skills.

_____ 1. cashier                  **a.** take care of patients

_____ 2. construction worker      **b.** drive a truck

_____ 3. nurse                     **c.** use a cash register

_____ 4. office assistant           **d.** build houses

_____ 5. truck driver               **e.** use a computer

**A** Write questions. Use *Where do* or *Where does*.

1. (he / work) _Where does he work?_____
2. (she / go to school) _____
3. (you / work) _____
4. (they / apply for the job) _____
5. (Emmy / drive a truck) _____

**B** Write questions and answers. Use *can*.

1. **A:** (you / use a computer) _Can you use a computer?_____
   **B:** Yes, _I can_____.
2. **A:** (she / speak two languages) _____
   **B:** No, _____.
3. **A:** (Tom / drive a truck) _____
   **B:** No, _____.
4. **A:** (they / build houses) _____
   **B:** Yes, _____.
5. **A:** (Laura / take care of patients) _____
   **B:** Yes, _____.
6. **A:** (you / use a cash register) _____
   **B:** No, _____.

# CONVERSATION REVIEW

**ROLE-PLAY.**

**Student A**
Apply for a server job. You can:

- help customers
- speak two languages
- work under pressure

**A:** Hello. I'm interested in the _____ position.

**B:** OK. What job skills do you have?

**A:** _____

**B:** Do you have any other skills?

**A:** _____

**B:** When can you work?

**A:** _____

**B:** Please fill out this application.

**A:** OK. Thank you.

**Student B**
Ask about Student A.

**Student B**
Apply for an office assistant job. You can:

- use a computer
- use office machines
- work with a team

**B:** Hello. I'm interested in the _____ position.

**A:** OK. What job skills do you have?

**B:** _____

**A:** Do you have any other skills?

**B:** _____

**A:** When can you work?

**B:** _____

**A:** Please fill out this application.

**B:** OK. Thank you.

**Student A**
Ask about Student B.

# LIFE SKILLS AND WRITING REVIEW

## 1 LIFE SKILLS: Fill out a job application

What kind of job are you interested in? Fill out the application.

● ● ●

**POSITION APPLYING FOR:** [_____]

**PERSONAL INFORMATION**

NAME [_____]        [_____]
        First                          Last

ADDRESS [_____]
        Street

[_____]        [___]  [_____]
City                              State   ZIP Code

[_____] - [_____] - [_____]
Phone Number

Are you 18 years or older?   ○ Yes   ○ No

---

**AVAILABILITY**

When can you begin work?   [_____] [_____] [_____]
                            Month   Day    Year

Are you interested in a full-time job or a part-time job?
○ FT    ○ PT

## 2 WRITE ABOUT YOURSELF

Complete the sentences.

1. My name is _____.
2. I'd like to apply for _____.
3. I can begin work _____.
4. I can work _____ hours a week.

**Unit Review:** Go back to page 213. Which unit goals can you check off?

# WORD LIST

## UNIT 1

Cambodia, 6
Canada, 6
China, 6
eight, 10
El Salvador, 6
five, 10

four, 10
Haiti, 6
Mexico, 6
nine, 10
one, 10
Peru, 6

seven, 10
six, 10
Somalia, 6
South Korea, 6
student, 14
Syria, 6

teacher, 14
three, 10
two, 10
United States, 6
Vietnam, 6
zero, 10

## UNIT 2

across from, 35
ask questions, 38
backpack, 28
book, 28
bookstore, 32
cafeteria, 32
classmates, 38
classroom, 32
close, 30
computer lab, 32

dictionary app, 28
eraser, 28
go to class, 38
library, 32
married, 36
Miss, 36
Mr. (mister), 36
Mrs. (missus), 36
Ms. (miss), 36
next to, 34

notebook, 28
office, 32
open, 30
paper, 28
pen, 28
pencil, 28
phone, 28
practice with my
   classmates, 38
put away, 30

read signs, 38
restroom, 32
single, 36
take out, 30
testing room, 32
turn off, 30
turn on, 30
use a dictionary app, 38
write new words, 38

## UNIT 3

eat breakfast, 52
eat lunch, 52
Friday, 54
get dressed, 52
get home, 52

get up, 52
go to school, 52
go to sleep, 52
go to work, 52
Monday, 54

numbers 0–59, 48
rest, 56
Saturday, 54
Sunday, 54
take a shower, 52

Thursday, 54
Tuesday, 54
Wednesday, 54

## UNIT 4

April, 72
August, 72
brother, 66
children, 66
clean the house, 70
daughter, 66
December, 72
do the laundry, 70
fall, 72

father, 66
February, 72
grandfather, 66
grandmother, 66
husband, 66
January, 72
July, 72
June, 72
make dinner, 70

March, 72
May, 72
months, 72
mother, 66
November, 72
October, 72
parents, 66
seasons, 72
September, 72

sister, 66
son, 66
spring, 72
summer, 72
take out the garbage, 70
vacuum, 70
wash the dishes, 70
wife, 66
winter, 72

## UNIT 5

aspirin, 90
batteries, 90
card, 94
cents, 92
deodorant, 90
dime, 86
dollar, 88

enter your PIN, 94
half-dollar, 86
insert your card, 94
light bulbs, 90
nickel, 86
paper towels, 90
penny, 86

quarter, 86
razors, 90
remove your card, 94
shampoo, 90
shaving cream, 90
sign your name, 94
soap, 90

swipe your card, 94
tap OK, 94
tissues, 90
toilet paper, 90
toothpaste, 90

## UNIT 6

apples, 108
bag, 111
baked potato, 114
bananas, 108
box, 111
can, 111
carrots, 104
cereal, 114
cheeseburger, 114
cherries, 108

chicken sandwich, 114
coffee, 114
cucumbers, 104
dozen, 111
eggs and toast, 114
French fries, 114
fruit salad, 114
gallon, 111
grapes, 108
green salad, 114

iced tea, 114
juice, 114
lettuce, 104
loaf, 111
mangoes, 108
mushrooms, 104
onions, 104
oranges, 108
pancakes, 114
peaches, 108

pears, 108
peas, 104
peppers, 104
potatoes, 104
pound, 110
rice, 114
strawberries, 108
tea, 114
tomatoes, 104
tuna fish sandwich, 114

## UNIT 7

avenue, 130
basement, 124

bathroom, 124
bed, 128

bedroom, 124
boulevard, 130

chair, 128
closet, 124

dining room, 124
dishwasher, 128
dresser, 128
drive, 130
dryer, 128
garage, 124
kitchen, 124

lamp, 128
lane, 130
large, 126
laundry room, 124
living room, 124
new, 126
refrigerator, 128

road, 130
shower, 128
sink, 128
small, 126
sofa, 128
stove, 128
street, 130

sunny, 126
table, 128
toilet, 128
washing machine, 128

## UNIT 8

beige, 146
black, 146
blue, 146
brown, 146
dress, 142
extra large, 144
gray, 146

green, 146
jacket, 142
jeans, 142
large, 144
medium, 144
orange, 146
pants, 142

pink, 146
purple, 146
red, 146
shirt, 142
shoes, 142
skirt, 142
small, 144

sneakers, 142
socks, 142
sweater, 142
T-shirt, 142
white, 146
yellow, 146

## UNIT 9

answer the phone, 166
count money, 166
do homework, 164
drive a truck, 166
exercise, 160
feed the cat, 164
fix cars, 166

go online, 160
go to the movies, 160
help a customer, 166
late, 168
listen to music, 160
look for something, 166
pay bills, 164

play soccer, 160
play the guitar, 160
play video games, 160
sick, 168
take a break, 166
take orders, 166
talk on the phone, 164

visit friends, 160
walk the dog, 164
wash the car, 164
watch TV, 160
work on the computer, 166

## UNIT 10

ATM, 178
bank, 178
bus stop, 178
carpool, 182
City Hall, 180
convenience store, 178
courthouse, 180
crosswalk, 186
Department of Motor
    Vehicles (DMV), 180
do not enter, 186

don't walk, 186
drive, 182
drugstore, 178
fire station, 180
go straight, 184
go two blocks, 184
hospital, 178
library, 180
no left turn, 186
no parking, 186
no U-turn, 186

one-way street, 186
park, 180
parking lot, 178
police station, 180
post office, 180
restaurant, 178
ride a bike, 182
school, 180
speed limit, 186
stop sign, 186
supermarket, 178

take a ferry, 182
take a taxi, 182
take the bus, 182
take the subway, 182
take the train, 182
turn left, 184
turn right, 184
walk, 182, 186

## UNIT 11

arm, 196
aspirin, 204
back, 196
backache, 200
breathe in, 198
breathe out, 198
capsules, 204
car accident, 202
chest, 196
cold, 200
cough, 200

cough syrup, 204
ear, 196
eye, 196
feet, 196
fever, 200
fire, 202
flu, 200
foot, 196
hand, 196
head, 196
headache, 200

heart attack, 202
knee, 196
leg, 196
lie down, 198
look straight ahead, 198
mouth, 196
neck, 196
nose, 196
open your mouth, 198
pills, 204
prescription medicine, 204

rob, 202
roll up your sleeves, 198
shoulder, 196
sit on the table, 198
sore throat, 200
step on the scale, 198
stomachache, 200
tablets, 204
take off your jacket, 198
teaspoon, 204
toothache, 200

## UNIT 12

apply online, 222
build houses, 218
bus driver, 214
cashier, 216
communicate well, 222
construction worker, 214
cook, 216
custodian, 216
dentist, 214
doctor, 216

factory worker, 216
fix something, 218
full-time, 222
help customers, 218
housekeeper, 214
in person, 222
independently, 222
manage time, 222
mechanic, 214
nurse, 216

nursing assistant, 214
office assistant, 216
operate machinery, 218
painter, 214
part-time, 222
positive attitude, 222
required, 222
sales assistant, 214
security guard, 216
server, 216

speak two languages, 218
take care of patients, 218
teacher's assistant, 214
team, 222
use a cash register, 218
use a computer, 218
use office machines, 218
weekdays, 222
weekends, 222
work under pressure, 222

# AUDIO SCRIPT

## UNIT 1

### Page 7, Conversation, Exercise A

**A:** Hello. My name is Rick Soto.
**B:** Hi. I'm May Chen.
**A:** Where are you from, May?
**B:** I'm from China.

### Page 8, Vocabulary, Exercise B

1. C
2. F
3. H
4. J
5. M
6. P
7. R
8. U
9. X
10. Z
11. L
12. Q

### Page 8, Vocabulary, Exercise D

1. hello, h-e-l-l-o
2. my, m-y
3. name, n-a-m-e
4. where, w-h-e-r-e
5. are, a-r-e
6. from, f-r-o-m

### Page 9, Conversation, Exercise A

**A:** What's your name, please?
**B:** Ana Sol.
**A:** Spell your first name.
**B:** A-N-A.
**A:** Spell your last name.
**B:** S-O-L.

### Page 10, Vocabulary, Exercise B

a. 0
b. 2
c. 5
d. 6
e. 8
f. 9

### Page 10, Vocabulary, Exercise C

1. The student ID is 02468.
2. The student ID is 65378.
3. The student ID is 05376.

### Page 11, Conversation, Exercise A

**A:** What's your student ID number?
**B:** 83241.
**A:** 83241?
**B:** That's right.

### Page 11, Conversation, Exercise C

**A:** What's your phone number?
**B:** 212-555-7169.
**A:** 212-555-7169?
**B:** That's right.

### Page 11, Conversation, Exercise E

1. 231-555-7283
2. 434-555-0516

### Page 11, Conversation, Exercise F

1. 813-555-6291
2. 325-555-0478
3. 714-555-3924

### Page 12, Grammar, Exercise C

1. I'm a student.
2. You're the teacher.
3. You're from Peru.
4. I'm from the United States.
5. I'm from Syria.
6. You're my classmate.

### Page 13, Conversation, Exercise A

**A:** Hello. I'm Rosa.
**B:** Hi. I'm Rick. Nice to meet you.
**A:** Nice to meet you, too.

### Page 14, Conversation, Exercise A

**A:** This is Jin Su. He is from Korea.
**B:** Hi, Jin Su. I'm Lora.
**C:** Nice to meet you.
**B:** Nice to meet you, too.

### Page 16, Conversation, Exercise A

**A:** Who are they?
**B:** Oscar and Carlos. They're my classmates.
**A:** Where are they from?
**B:** They're from Brazil.

### Page 18, Reading, Exercise A

first name
middle name
last name
phone number
place of birth
student ID number

### Page 20, Listening, Exercise B
### Page 21, Reading, Exercise A

This is Ivan. He is a student.

He says hello to his classmates and smiles.

In his school, some students say hello and shake hands.

Some students say hello and hug.
Some students say hello and bow.
Other students say hello and kiss.

## UNIT 2

### Page 29, Conversation, Exercise A

**A:** Excuse me. Do you have a pencil?
**B:** No, I don't.
**A:** Do you have a pen?
**B:** Yes, I do. Here you go.
**A:** Thanks.

### Page 31, Conversation, Exercise A

**A:** It is time for a test. Please close your books.
**B:** OK.
**A:** Use a pencil. Don't use a pen.

### Page 31, Grammar, Exercise B

1. Don't open your backpack.
2. Don't use a dictionary app.
3. Don't put away your notebook.
4. Don't turn off your phone.
5. Don't take out your book.
6. Don't close the door.

### Page 33, Conversation, Exercise A

**A:** Where is the teacher?
**B:** He's in the library.

### Page 33, Conversation, Exercise D

1. Where is the teacher?
   He's in the computer lab.
2. Where is Sara?
   She's in the library.
3. Where is your book?
   It's in the cafeteria.
4. Where is your backpack?
   It's in the classroom.

### Page 34, Conversation, Exercise A

**A:** Excuse me. Where is the bookstore?
**B:** It's next to the testing room.
**A:** Thanks.

### Page 35, Conversation, Exercise A

**A:** Excuse me. Where is the library?
**B:** It's across from the office.
**A:** Thanks.

### Page 36, Vocabulary, Exercise B

1. Mrs. Chen
2. Mr. Smith
3. Ms. Lopez
4. Miss Park

### Page 36, Reading, Exercise A

Mr.
Mrs.
Miss
Ms.
last name
first name
place of birth
female
male
class
teacher

### Page 38, Conversation, Exercise A

**A:** How do you study English?
**B:** I practice with my classmates, and I write new words.
**A:** That's great!

### Page 40, Listening, Exercise B
### Page 41, Reading, Exercise A

This is Lan.
In her native country, students do not talk in class.
They listen to the teacher.
In the United States, students talk in groups.
Students ask questions.
The teacher listens to the students.

## UNIT 3

### Page 48, Vocabulary, Exercise C

a. 20
b. 19
c. 24
d. 13
e. 15
f. 14
g. 26
h. 27

### Page 49, Conversation, Exercise A

**A:** What time is it?
**B:** It's 1:00.

## Page 50, Conversation, Exercise A

**A:** What time is your English class?
**B:** It's from 9:00 to 12:30.
**A:** What time is your break?
**B:** It's from 10:45 to 11:15.

## Page 53, Conversation, Exercise A

**A:** What time do you go to work?
**B:** I go to work at 6:00. What time do you go to work?
**A:** I go to work at 10:00.

## Page 54, Conversation, Exercise A

**A:** When do you work, Nora?
**B:** I work from Monday to Friday.
**A:** When do you go to school?
**B:** I go to school on Saturday.
**A:** You're really busy!

## Page 54, Conversation, Exercise C

Hi, I'm Nora. I'm very busy. I work from Monday to Friday. I go to school on Saturday. I go to the library on Sunday.

## Page 55, Grammar, Exercise B

1. I work from Monday to Thursday.
2. We play soccer on Tuesday.
3. I go to school on Friday.
4. They go to school from Wednesday to Friday.
5. I eat lunch at home on Sunday.

## Page 58, Listening, Exercise B
## Page 59, Reading, Exercise A

Manny gets up at 6:00.

He gets to work at 7:55. He starts work at 8:00. He is on time.

He goes to school after work.

He gets to class at 5:45. Class starts at 6:00. He is early.

Manny meets friends on Saturday. But he is late!

## Page 61, Vocabulary Review, Exercise A

1. 46
2. 16
3. 81
4. 25
5. 38
6. 73
7. 2
8. 57
9. 11
10. 99

# UNIT 4

## Page 67, Conversation, Exercise A

**A:** Who's that?
**B:** That's my brother.
**A:** What's his name?
**B:** Sam.
**A:** Who's that?
**B:** That's my sister.
**A:** What's her name?
**B:** Her name is Tina.

## Page 68, Conversation, Exercise A

**A:** Do you have any sisters or brothers?
**B:** Yes. I have two sisters and one brother.
**A:** That's nice. Do you have any children?
**B:** No, I don't.

## Page 68, Reading, Exercise A

Hi, I'm Marta. This is my family. That's my husband. His name is Pedro. My parents are Linda and Roberto. I have two sons, Ernesto and Tino. I have one daughter. Her name is Ana.

## Page 69, Grammar, Exercise A

one brother, two brothers
a sister, three sisters
one son, two sons
a daughter, three daughters
one parent, two parents
one child, two children

## Page 71, Conversation, Exercise A

**A:** Do you vacuum?
**B:** Yes, I do.
**A:** Do you make dinner?
**B:** No, I don't.

## Page 72, Vocabulary, Exercise B

1. December
2. June
3. October
4. January
5. May
6. April

## Page 73, Conversation, Exercise A

**A:** What's your favorite season?
**B:** Summer.
**A:** That's nice. My favorite season is spring.

## Page 74, Vocabulary, Exercise D

1. February 23, 1994
2. July 14, 2015
3. September 2, 2009
4. January 11, 2019
5. September 7, 1974

## Page 75, Conversation, Exercise A

**A:** What is today's date?
**B:** April 9, 2019.
**A:** Thanks.

## Page 76, Reading, Exercise A

first name
middle name
last name
today's date
date of birth
place of birth
class
teacher
class schedule
day
time
room

## Page 78, Listening, Exercise B
## Page 79, Reading, Exercise A

Lucas and Carla are married. Lucas is Carla's husband. Carla is Lucas's wife.

In their native country, men go to work.

In their native country, women do the household chores.

In the United States, Carla and Lucas go to work.

They both do household chores. Lucas washes the dishes.

Lucas goes to the supermarket, too.

## Page 81, Vocabulary Review, Exercise B

1. January
2. February
3. March
4. April
5. May
6. June
7. July
8. August
9. September
10. October
11. November
12. December

## UNIT 5

## Page 86, Conversation, Exercise A

**A:** Excuse me. Do you have change for a dollar?
**B:** Yes. I have two quarters and five dimes. Here you go.
**A:** Thanks.

## Page 87, Conversation, Exercise D

1. Do you have change for a dollar?
   Yes. I have three quarters, two dimes, and a nickel.
2. Do you have change for a dollar?
   Yes. I have two quarters, four dimes, and two nickels.
3. Do you have change for a quarter?
   Yes. I have a dime and three nickels.
4. Do you have change for a quarter?
   Yes. I have two dimes and five pennies.

## Page 89, Conversation, Exercise A

**A:** Excuse me. Do you have change for a ten?
**B:** Yes. I have a five and five ones. Here you go.
**A:** Great.

## Page 89, Conversation, Exercise D

1. Do you have change for a five?
   Yes. I have five ones.
2. Do you have change for a twenty?
   Yes. I have two tens.
3. Do you have change for a fifty?
   Yes. I have two twenties and two fives.
4. Do you have change for a hundred?
   Yes. I have a fifty, two twenties, and a ten.

## Page 91, Grammar, Exercise B

1. Where is the shampoo?
2. Where are the paper towels?
3. Where is the shaving cream?
4. Where are the light bulbs?
5. Where are the batteries?

## Page 92, Vocabulary, Exercise B

1. It's 17 cents.
2. It's 36 cents.
3. It's 44 cents.
4. It's 60 cents.
5. It's 79 cents.
6. It's 95 cents.

## Page 92, Vocabulary, Exercise D

1. It's $1.25.
2. It's $3.07.
3. It's $4.79.
4. It's $7.50.
5. It's $8.99.
6. It's $10.42.
7. It's $12.55.
8. It's $15.35.
9. It's $17.95.

## Page 93, Conversation, Exercise A

**A:** Excuse me. How much is the toothpaste?
**B:** It's $3.99.
**A:** How much are the batteries?
**B:** They're $4.50.
**A:** Thanks.

## Page 96, Listening, Exercise B
## Page 97, Reading, Exercise A

This is Edna. In her native country, she shops at a market.

She talks about the price. She asks for a better price.

She is happy.

In the United States, Edna shops in a big store.

Each item has one price.

Edna pays a good price in the United States, too. She buys things on sale.

## UNIT 6

## Page 105, Conversation, Exercise A

**A:** Hi. I'm at the store. Do we need vegetables?
**B:** Yes. We need tomatoes and carrots.
**A:** OK. Do we need onions?
**B:** No. We have onions.

## Page 105, Conversation, Exercise D

Hi, I'm Pam. It's time to make vegetable soup! I have tomatoes, onions, peas, and potatoes. I need mushrooms and carrots.

## Page 106, Conversation, Exercises A, B, and C

**A:** Do you like vegetables?
**B:** I like tomatoes. I don't like onions. What about you?
**A:** I like peppers. I don't like carrots.

## Page 109, Conversation, Exercise A

**A:** Does your daughter like fruit?
**B:** She likes apples. She doesn't like pears.

## Page 110, Vocabulary

bananas, one ninety-nine a pound
grapes, three seventy-nine a pound
fish, eight ninety-nine a pound
ground beef, five eighty-nine a pound
chicken, four thirty-nine a pound

## Page 110, Conversation, Exercise A

**A:** Do you need anything from the store?
**B:** Yes. I need one pound of grapes and two pounds of ground beef.

## Page 111, Conversation, Exercise A

**A:** What do we need from the store?
**B:** We need a bag of rice and two dozen eggs.

## Page 112, Reading, Exercise A

Shop Mart Weekly Specials
a loaf of bread, $1.79
one dozen eggs, $1.29
chicken, $1.99 a pound
tomato soup, 79 cents. buy one, get one free.
cereal, $4.25
bananas, 49 cents a pound

## Page 115, Conversation, Exercise A

**A:** Are you ready to order?
**B:** Yes. I'd like a tuna fish sandwich, a green salad, and an iced tea.
**A:** Anything else?
**B:** No, thank you.

## Page 116, Listening, Exercise B
## Page 117, Reading, Exercise A

This is Tran. In his native country, most people eat with chopsticks.

Many children eat with their hands.

This is Riko. In her native country, many people drink soup.

In the United States, most people eat with a fork, knife, and spoon.

They eat sandwiches and French fries with their hands.

## Page 122, Life Skills Review, Exercise A

a bag of rice
a dozen eggs
a pound of ground beef
two pounds of chicken

## UNIT 7

## Page 125, Conversation, Exercise A

**A:** Guess what? I have a new apartment.
**B:** Really? What's it like?
**A:** It has a kitchen, a living room, and one bedroom.
**B:** It sounds great!

## Page 126, Conversation, Exercise A

**A:** Can you tell me about the apartment for rent?

**B:** There is a sunny bedroom, a new kitchen, and a large living room.

**A:** It sounds nice.

## Page 129, Conversation, Exercise A

**A:** I have some questions about the apartment. Is there a refrigerator?

**B:** Yes, there is.

**A:** Are there any lamps?

**B:** No, there aren't.

## Page 129, Grammar, Exercise B

1. Is there a stove?
   Yes, there is.

2. Are there any chairs?
   Yes, there are.

3. Are there any lamps?
   No, there aren't.

4. Is there a washing machine?
   No, there isn't.

## Page 130, Vocabulary, Exercise B

1. 270 John Lane
2. 15 City Street
3. 1460 Third Avenue
4. 60 Park Drive
5. 319 Sun Boulevard

## Page 130, Vocabulary, Exercise C

1. 75 Sandy Boulevard
2. 1325 West Avenue
3. 5 Main Street
4. 836 Jones Road
5. 1514 North Drive
6. 26 Town Lane

## Page 131, Conversation, Exercise A

**A:** I'm looking for an apartment.

**B:** Oh! There's an apartment for rent on my street.

**A:** What's the address?

**B:** It's 1630 River Street.

**A:** How much is the rent?

**B:** It's $900 a month.

## Page 134, Listening, Exercise B
## Page 135, Reading, Exercise A

This is Pilar. She is 21 years old. She is single.

Pilar lives with her sister and her sister's husband.

Pilar has a good job. She works in an office.

Pilar wants to live with her friends. In the United States, many single people live with friends.

Pilar's parents are not happy. In their native country, single people live with their families.

# UNIT 8

## Page 143, Conversation, Exercise A

**A:** Let's go shopping! I need a new jacket.

**B:** OK. I need new shoes.

## Page 144, Conversation, Exercise A

**A:** Can I help you?

**B:** Do you have this shirt in large?

**A:** Yes. Here you go.

**B:** Do you have these pants in size 12?

**A:** No, I'm sorry. We don't.

## Page 147, Conversation, Exercise A

**A:** Is Nina here?

**B:** Yes. She's over there.

**A:** Where? What does she have on?

**B:** She has on a red shirt and black pants.

**A:** OK. Thanks.

## Page 148, Vocabulary, Exercise B

1. This shirt is too big.
2. Those pants are too small.
3. This dress is too big.
4. Those sneakers are too small.

## Page 148, Conversation, Exercise A

**A:** I need to return this jacket and these shoes.

**B:** What's the problem?

**A:** The jacket is too big. The shoes are too small. Here's my receipt.

## Page 151, Writing, Exercise A

Dan's Clothing Store.

Sale! February 16–18.

Sweaters, regular price $35.99, on sale for $25.99.

Pants, regular price $29, on sale for $15.99.

T-shirts, regular price $15.50, on sale for $10.

Shoes, regular price $52.99, on sale for $45.

Sneakers, regular price $40.99, on sale for $25.

Jackets, regular price $75, on sale for $50.

**Page 152, Listening, Exercise B**
**Page 153, Reading, Exercise A**

This is Yun. She lives in the United States. She is getting married.

Her wedding is in August. She needs a new dress. She wants a white dress.

In her native country, people wear white clothes at funerals.

Many women wear a red and green dress at their wedding.

Yun's mother and grandmother want her to have a red and green dress.

## UNIT 9

**Page 161, Conversation, Exercise A**

**A:** What do you do in your free time?
**B:** I listen to music. What do you do?
**A:** I play soccer.
**B:** How often?
**A:** Once a week.

**Page 162, Conversation, Exercise A**

**A:** Hello?
**B:** Hi, Sara. It's Bill. What are you doing?
**A:** I'm watching a movie. Can I call you later?
**B:** No problem. Bye.
**A:** Goodbye.

**Page 163, Grammar, Exercise C**

1. What are you doing?
   I'm listening to music.
2. What is Mrs. White doing?
   She's going online.
3. What are you doing?
   We're visiting friends.
4. What's Rob doing?
   He's watching a movie.
5. Ware are Amy and David doing?
   They're playing video games.

**Page 164, Conversation, Exercise A**

**A:** Hello?
**B:** Hi, Jin. How's everything going?
**A:** Great.
**B:** Is Alex doing the laundry?
**A:** Yes, he is.
**B:** Is Tina washing the car?
**A:** No, she's not. She's talking on the phone!

**Page 167, Grammar, Exercise B**

1. She's driving a truck.
2. She's not helping a customer.
3. He's counting money.
4. He's not answering the phone.
5. They're taking a break.
6. They're not taking orders.
7. She's answering the phone.
8. She's not fixing cars.

**Page 168, Reading, Exercise A**

**A:** This is Dan Green. Please leave a message.
**B:** Hi, Dan. This is Victor Mata. I'm sorry, but I'm not coming to work today. I'm sick.

**Page 169, Reading, Exercise C**

**A:** This is Dan Green. Please leave a message.
**B:** Hi, Dan. This is Tanya Smith. I'm sorry, but I'm late for work. My bus is late.

**Page 170, Listening, Exercise B**
**Page 171, Reading, Exercise A**

This is Luis. He lives in the United States. He has two children.

His children are busy on weekends. They talk to their friends. They play sports.

Luis and his wife eat alone on weekends. Their children are busy every Saturday and Sunday.

In Luis's native country, families are together on weekends.

They spend time together. They talk.

**Page 176, Life Skills Review, Exercise A**

Monday: work, school
Tuesday: work
Wednesday: work, school
Thursday: work
Friday: work, movies
Saturday: soccer
Sunday: make dinner

## UNIT 10

**Page 179, Vocabulary, Exercise C**

First Street
Second Street
Third Street
Central Avenue
Main Avenue
Grand Avenue

## Page 179, Conversation, Exercise A

**A:** Excuse me. Is there a bank near here?
**B:** Yes. There's a bank on the corner of First Street and Central Avenue.
**A:** Thank you.

## Page 181, Conversation

**A:** Excuse me. Where is City Hall?
**B:** It's between the police station and the DMV.
**A:** Between the police station and the DMV?
**B:** Yes. And it's across from the park.

## Page 183, Conversation, Exercise A

**A:** Hi, Ben. Where are you going?
**B:** I'm going to work.
**A:** Oh. How do you get to work?
**B:** I take the bus.

## Page 183, Conversation, Exercise C

Ed is a student. He goes to school on Monday and Wednesday. His school is on the corner of White Street and Second Avenue. It's next to the park. He takes the bus to school.

## Page 184, Vocabulary, Exercise B

1. Where the bank?
   It's on Park Street. Go straight for one block.
2. Where's the post office?
   It's between the DMV and City Hall. Turn left on Third Street.
3. Where's the school?
   It's on Lake Street. Turn right at the corner.
4. Where's the hospital?
   It's on First Street. Turn right at the corner.
5. Where's the convenience store?
   Turn left at the bank. It's next to the drugstore.
6. Where's the police station?
   Go two blocks. It's across from the park.

## Page 184. Vocabulary, Exercise C

1. Is there a bank near here?
   Yes. Go straight. It's on the corner of Third Avenue and Church Street.
2. Where's the hospital?
   Go straight for three blocks and turn right. It's on the corner of First Avenue and Bank Street.
3. Where's the drugstore?
   Go to Third Avenue and turn right at the corner. Go straight for two blocks.
4. Is there a post office near here?
   Yes. Go straight for two blocks. Turn right at the corner. It's on the corner of Second Avenue and Bank Street.

5. Is there a school near here?
   Go straight for two blocks. Turn left at the corner. It's on the corner of Second Avenue and White Street.

## Page 185, Conversation, Exercise A

**A:** Excuse me. Where is the train station?
**B:** It's on Park Street. Go straight for one block. Then turn left on Park Street.
**A:** Thanks a lot!

## Page 187, Vocabulary, Exercise C

1. no parking
2. no U-turn
3. crosswalk
4. stop
5. do not enter
6. speed limit 25 miles per hour

## Page 187, Reading, Exercise A

1. Only go one way on this street.
2. Don't walk across the street.
3. Stop at the corner.
4. Drive 25 miles per hour.

## Page 188, Listening, Exercise B
## Page 189, Reading, Exercise A

This is Mohammed.

In Mohammed's native country, he takes the bus to get to work.

He takes the subway to get to English class.

He takes a taxi to go shopping.

Mohammed lives in the United States. He has a car.

In the United States, Mohammed drives to work. He drives to English class. He drives to go shopping.

## UNIT 11

## Page 197, Conversation, Exercise A

**A:** Hello. Westside Health Clinic.
**B:** This is Tom Perez. I'd like to make an appointment.
**A:** What's the problem?
**B:** My back hurts.
**A:** Can you come in at 4:00?
**B:** Yes, I can.

## Page 199, Conversation, Exercise A

**A:** Hello. I'm Dr. Medina. Why are you here today?
**B:** I'm here for a checkup.
**A:** OK. Sit on the table. Look straight ahead.

**Page 199, Conversation, Exercise C**

Isabel gets a checkup every year. She goes to the health clinic. Her appointment is on Monday. Her doctor says, "You are healthy."

**Page 200, Vocabulary, Exercises A and B**

a headache
a backache
a stomachache
a toothache
a cold
a cough
a fever
the flu
a sore throat

**Page 201, Conversation, Exercise A**

**A:** What's the matter?
**B:** I have a cold.
**A:** You should drink a lot of liquids.

**Page 203, Conversation, Exercise A**

**A:** 911. What's your emergency?
**B:** My friend is having a heart attack.
**A:** Where are you?
**B:** 1038 Park Avenue.
**A:** What's the cross street?
**B:** River Road.

**Page 204, Vocabulary, Exercise B**

**Conversation 1**
Are you OK? You have a bad cough.
I know. I'm taking cough syrup.
How much are you taking?
I'm taking two teaspoons every four hours.
I hope you feel better soon.

**Conversation 2**
Hi, Mike. How are you?
I don't feel well. I have a fever and an ear infection.
Oh that's too bad. Are you taking medicine?
Yes. I'm taking some prescription medicine.
That's good. How often do you take it?
I have to take one capsule twice a day with food.
I hope you feel better soon.

**Page 206, Listening, Exercise B**
**Page 207, Reading, Exercise A**

This is Teresa. She is 45 years old.

In Teresa's native country, people go to the doctor when they are sick.

Teresa lives in the United States. Her daughter wants her to get a checkup.

Her daughter says people should go to the doctor every year.

Teresa feels healthy. She does not want to get a checkup.

## UNIT 12

**Page 215, Conversation, Exercise A**

**A:** Let's get coffee.
**B:** I'm sorry. I can't. I have to go to work.
**A:** Oh. What do you do?
**B:** I'm a teacher's assistant.

**Page 217, Conversation, Exercise A**

**A:** Who's that?
**B:** That's Bo. He's a nurse.
**A:** Where does he work?
**B:** He works at Valley Hospital.

**Page 219, Conversation, Exercise A**

**A:** What are your job skills?
**B:** I can use a computer. And I can use a cash register.
**A:** What other skills do you have?
**B:** I can speak two languages.

**Page 219, Conversation, Exercise C**

Grace needs a new job. She has an interview on Wednesday. Grace has many skills. She can use a computer and a cash register. Grace can also speak two languages.

**Page 220, Conversation, Exercise A**

**A:** Hello. I'd like to apply for the office assistant job.
**B:** OK. Can you use a computer?
**A:** Yes, I can.
**B:** Please fill out the application.
**A:** Thank you.

**Page 221, Grammar, Exercise B**

1. Can Miss Tang serve customers?
   Yes, she can.
2. Can Mr. Black use a computer?
   No, he can't.
3. Can you build houses?
   Yes, I can.
4. Can Marina and Pedro help customers?
   Yes, they can.
5. Can Ella speak two languages?
   No, she can't.

**Page 224, Listening, Exercise B**

**Page 225, Reading, Exercise A**

This is Monika. She lives in the United States.

Monika has a job interview on Thursday at 9:00.

Monika is ready for the interview. She practiced her interview skills in her English class.

Monika gets to the interview. She is early. She says hello and smiles.

She shakes hands with Mr. Cruz.

Mr. Cruz asks about Monika's job skills. She answers his questions.

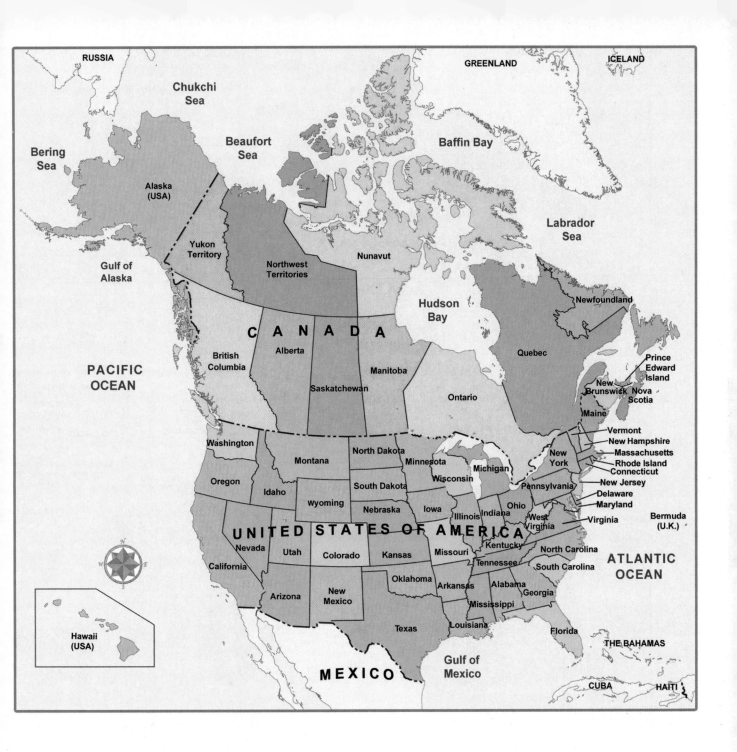

RUSSIA

Chukchi
Sea

GREENLAND

ICELAND

Bering
Sea

Beaufort
Sea

Baffin Bay

Alaska
(USA)

Gulf of
Alaska

Yukon
Territory

Northwest
Territories

Nunavut

Labrador
Sea

PACIFIC
OCEAN

C A N A D A

British
Columbia

Alberta

Saskatchewan

Manitoba

Hudson
Bay

Ontario

Quebec

Newfoundland

Prince
Edward
Island
New
Brunswick Nova
Scotia
Maine

Washington

Montana

North Dakota

Minnesota

Michigan

Wisconsin

New
York

Vermont
New Hampshire
Massachusetts
Rhode Island
Connecticut
New Jersey
Delaware
Maryland

Oregon

Idaho

wyoming

South Dakota

Nebraska

Iowa

Illinois

Indiana

Ohio

Pennsylvania

West
Virginia

Virginia

Bermuda
(U.K.)

UNITED STATES OF AMERICA

Nevada

Utah

Colorado

Kansas

Missouri

Kentucky

ATLANTIC
OCEAN

California

Arizona

New
Mexico

Oklahoma

Tennessee

North Carolina

South Carolina

Arkansas

Alabama

Georgia

Mississippi

Texas

Louisiana

Florida

THE BAHAMAS

Hawaii
(USA)

MEXICO

Gulf of
Mexico

CUBA

HAITI

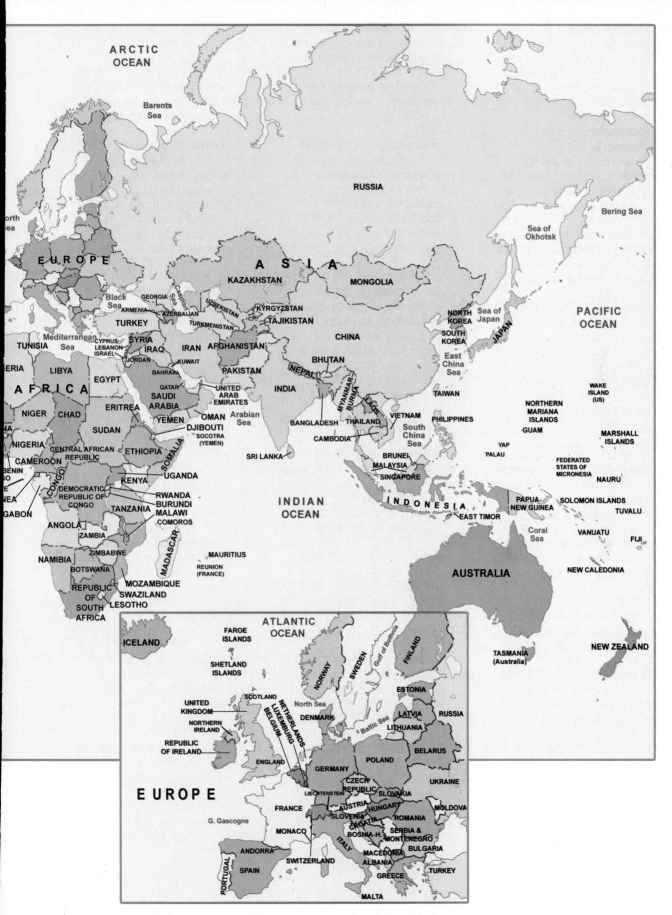

# INDEX

**Photos:**

**Front cover:** Front cover: Westend61/Getty Images; Bjoern Lauen/ArabianEye/Getty Images; Hero Images/Getty Images; Manuel Breva Colmeiro/Moment/Getty Images.

**Frontmatter**

Page vi (cellphone): Tele52/Shutterstock; vi (front cover): Westend61/Getty Images; vi (front cover): Bjoern Lauen/ArabianEye/Getty Images; vi (front cover): Hero Images/Getty Images; vi (front cover): Manuel Breva Colmeiro/Moment/Getty Images; vi (MyEnglishLab screenshot): Pearson Education Inc.; vi (ActiveTeach screenshot): Pearson Education Inc.; vi (CCRS page, bottom left): Wavebreakmedia/Shutterstock; vi (CCRS page, top, right): Illustration Forest/Shutterstock; vi Wavebreak Media Ltd/123RF (Active Teach page); vii: Siri Stafford/DigitalVision/Getty Images; viii (left, p. 66): Shutterstock; viii (right, p. 67): Dmytro Zinkevych/123RF; ix (p. 68): Wavebreak Media Ltd/123RF; x (p. 76): rSnapshotPhotos/Shutterstock; xiii (p. 81 [1]): Kirill Kedrinski/123RF; xiii (p. 81 [2]): Maskot/Getty Images; xiii (p. 81 [3]): Andriy Popov/123RF; xiii (p. 81 [4]): Hongqi Zhang/123RF; xiii (p. 81 [5]): Elena Elisseeva/Shutterstock; xiii (p. 81 [6]): Andriy Popov/123RF; xiii (p. 83): Cathy Yeulet/123RF; xxii: Courtesy of Sarah Lynn; xxii: Courtesy of Ronna Magy; xxii: Courtesy of Federico Salas Isnardi.

**Pre-unit: Welcome to Class**
Page 4: Tele52/Shutterstock.

**Unit 1**

Page 5: Dolgachov/123RF; 7: Thomas Barwick/DigitalVision/Getty Images; 9: AshTproductions/Shutterstock; 10 (John Pace): Comstock/Stockbyte/Getty Images; 10 (John Potter): Joe Belanger/Shutterstock; 10 (Sue Gao): Fuse/Corbis/Getty Images; 10 (Grace Tang): Ariwasabi/123RF; 10 (Anne Joseph): OLJ Studio/Shutterstock; 10 (Anne Crane): Arek_Malang/Shutterstock; 11: Jörg Carstensen/Pearson Education Ltd; 12 (left): Original Photography by David Mager; 12 (right): Original Photography by David Mager; 13: Blend Images/Shutterstock; 14 (A, left): Elwynn/123RF; 14 (A, right): Iofoto/Shutterstock; 14 (B, 1): Tracy Whiteside/Shutterstock; 14 (B, 2): Simon Greig/Shutterstock; 14 (B, 3): Leungchopan/Shutterstock; 14 (B, 4): Shutterstock; 14 (B, 5): Phase4Studios/Shutterstock; 14 (B, 6): SnowWhiteimages/Shutterstock; 14 (bottom, right): James Hardy/PhotoAlto/Alamy Stock Photo; 15 (1): Christopher Meder/Shutterstock; 15 (2): Darrin Henry/123RF; 15 (3): Blend Images/Shutterstock; 15 (4): Mimagephotography/Shutterstock; 16 (1): Original Photography by David Mager; 16 (2): Original Photography by David Mager; 16 (3): Original Photography by David Mager; 23 (1): Cathy Yeulet/123RF; 23 (2): David Gilder/Shutterstock; 23 (3): OLJ Studio/Shutterstock; 25: Sirtravelalot/Shutterstock.

**Unit 2**

Page 27: Robert Kneschke/Shutterstock; 28 (1): Rabia Elif Aksoy/123RF; 28 (2): Bondarchuk/Shutterstock; 28 (3): Valkr/Shutterstock; 28 (4): Joe Belanger/Shutterstock; 28 (5): Binik/Shutterstock; 28 (6): Weerachai Ruttanasopa/Shutterstock; 28 (7): Vitaly Korovin/123RF; 28 (8): Olegdudko/123RF; 28 (9): J. Helgason/Shutterstock; 29: VP Photo Studio/Shutterstock; 31: Wavebreakmedia/Shutterstock; 32 (1): Wavebreakmedia/Shutterstock; 32 (2): Trekandshoot/Shutterstock; 32 (3): Jack Hollingsworth/Photodisc/Getty Images; 32 (4): Dumrongsak/123RF; 32 (5): Sakaekrung/Shutterstock; 32 (6): Hotsum/Shutterstock; 32 (7): Mint Images/Getty Images; 32 (8): Picsfive/Shutterstock; 33: Wavebreak Media Ltd/123RF; 36 (left, top): Stylephotographs/123RF; 36 (left, bottom): Blend Images/Shutterstock; 38 (1): Rabia Elif Aksoy/123RF; 38 (2): Maskot/Getty Images; 38 (3): Wavebreak Media Ltd/123RF; 38 (4): Frederic Cirou/PhotoAlto/Alamy Stock Photo; 38 (5): ESB Professional/Shutterstock; 38 (6): Clynt Garnham Education/Alamy Stock Photo; 38 (bottom, left): Michaeljung/Shutterstock; 39: Blend Images/Shutterstock; 43 (1): Fotocrisis/Shutterstock; 43 (2): Ekaphon Maneechot/Shutterstock; 43 (3): Newphotoservice/Shutterstock; 43 (4): Kongsak Yonyot/123RF; 43 (5): Bryljaev/123RF; 43 (6): Cheuk-King Lo/Pearson Education Asia Ltd; 43 (7): Jean-Marie Guyon/123RF; 43 (8): John Arehart/Shutterstock.

**Unit 3**

Page 47: Mangostar/Shutterstock; 48 (D): Maxfromhell/Shutterstock; 50 (top, left): Frederic Cirou/PhotoAlto Agency RF Collections/Getty Images; 50 (top, center): Klaus Vedfelt/DigitalVision/Getty Images; 50 (bottom, right): Ammentorp/123RF; 52 (1): Lightwavemedia/Shutterstock; 52 (2): Di Studio/Shutterstock; 52 (3): FLUKY FLUKY/Shutterstock; 52 (4): Zohaib Hussain/Getty Images; 52 (5): Dolgachov/123RF; 52 (6): Wong Yu Liang/123RF; 52 (7): Stieberszabolcs/123RF; 52 (8): Shutterstock; 52 (9): Andriy Popov/123RF; 53 (top, left): John M Lund Photography Inc/DigitalVision/Getty Images; 53 (top, right): Lena Mirisola/Image Source/

Getty Images; 54: Wavebreak Media Ltd/123RF; 56 (top, left): Tele52/Shutterstock; 56 (top, right): Cathy Yeulet/123RF; 57: Tele52/Shutterstock; 61 (1): Wavebreak Media Ltd/123RF; 61 (2): Di Studio/Shutterstock; 61 (3): S_L/Shutterstock; 61 (4): Cathy Yeulet/123RF; 61 (5): Darrin Henry/Shutterstock; 61 (6): Cathy Yeulet/123RF.

**Unit 4**

Page 65: Siri Stafford/DigitalVision/Getty Images; 66: Shutterstock; 67: Dmytro Zinkevych/123RF; 68: Wavebreak Media Ltd/123RF; 70 (1): Torwai Suebsri/123RF; 70 (2): Dinis Tolipov/123RF; 70 (3): Thanapol Kuptanisakorn/123RF; 70 (4): Andriy Popov/123RF; 70 (5): Andriy Popov/123RF; 70 (6): TinnaPong/Shutterstock; 71 (left): Beeboys/Shutterstock; 71 (right): Catalin Petolea/Shutterstock; 72 (spring): Olena Z/Shutterstock; 72 (summer): Lotus_studio/Shutterstock; 72 (fall): Dean Fikar/Shutterstock; 72 (winter): John A. Anderson/Shutterstock; 75: Selinofoto/Shutterstock; 76: rSnapshotPhotos/Shutterstock; 81(1): Kirill Kedrinski/123RF; 81(2): Maskot/Getty Images; 81 (3): Andriy Popov/123RF; 81(4): Hongqi Zhang/123RF; 81 (5): Elena Elisseeva/Shutterstock; 81 (6): Andriy Popov/123RF; 83: Cathy Yeulet/123RF.

**Unit 5**

Page 85: ColorBlind/The Image Bank/Getty Images; 86 (penny): B Brown/Shutterstock; 86 (nickel): B Brown/Shutterstock; 86 (dime): B Brown/Shutterstock; 86 (quarter): B Brown/Shutterstock; 86 (half dollar): Andrei Kuzmik/Shutterstock; 87 (penny): B Brown/Shutterstock; 87 (nickel): B Brown/Shutterstock; 87 (dime): B Brown/Shutterstock; 87 (quarter): B Brown/Shutterstock; 88 (one dollar): Onehundred Percent/Alamy Stock Photo; 88 (five dollars): Jonny White/Alamy Stock Photo; 88 (ten dollars): Onehundred Percent/Alamy Stock Photo; 88 (twenty dollars): Art-Studio/Alamy Stock Photo; 88 (fifty dollars): Onehundred Percent/Alamy Stock Photo; 88 (one hundred dollars): Pius Koller/ImageBROKER/Alamy Stock Photo; 89 (top, right): Original Photography by David Mager; 89 (one dollar): Onehundred Percent/Alamy Stock Photo; 89 (ten dollars): Onehundred Percent/Alamy Stock Photo; 89 (five dollars): Jonny White/Alamy Stock Photo; 89 (twenty dollars): Art-Studio/Alamy Stock Photo; 89 (fifty dollars): Onehundred Percent/Alamy Stock Photo; 90 (1): Jiri Hera/Shutterstock; 90 (2): Sergey Kolesnikov/123RF; 90 (3): Jane Waterbury/123RF; 90 (4): Alexandr Vlassyuk/Shutterstock; 90 (5): Leah-Anne Thompson/Shutterstock; 90 (6): Jvart/123RF; 90 (7): Sergey Soldatov/123RF; 90 (8): Somchai Somsanitangkul/123RF; 90 (9): Mihalec/Shutterstock; 90 (10): Hurst Photo/Shutterstock; 90 (11): Murat Baysan/123RF; 90 (12): Pixelrobot/Shutterstock; 91: Iakov Filimonov/123RF; 93 (top): Dragon Images/Shutterstock; 93 (soap): Jiri Hera/Shutterstock; 93 (tissues): Pixelrobot/Shutterstock; 93 (deodorant): Sergey Kolesnikov/123RF; 93 (light bulbs): Somchai Somsanitangkul/123RF; 93 (aspirin): Hurst Photo/Shutterstock; 93 (razors): Murat Baysan/123RF; 99 (half dollar): Andrei Kuzmik/Shutterstock; 99 (penny): B Brown/Shutterstock; 99 (quarter): B Brown/Shutterstock; 99 (dime): B Brown/Shutterstock; 99 (nickel): B Brown/Shutterstock; 99 (one hundred dollars): Pius Koller/ImageBROKER/Alamy Stock Photo; 99 (fifty dollars): Onehundred Percent/Alamy Stock Photo; 99 (twenty dollars): Art-Studio/Alamy Stock Photo; 99 (ten dollars): Onehundred Percent/Alamy Stock Photo; 99 (five dollars): Jonny White/Alamy Stock Photo; 99 (one dollar): Onehundred Percent/Alamy Stock Photo; 101 (soap):Jiri Hera/Shutterstock; 101 (paper towels): Alexandr Vlassyuk/Shutterstock; 101 (shampoo): Mihalec/Shutterstock; 101 (light bulbs): Somchai Somsanitangkul/123RF; 101 (toothpaste): Leah-Anne Thompson/Shutterstock; 101 (notebooks): Siraphol/123RF.

**Unit 6**

Page 103: Rawpixel.com/Shutterstock; 104 (1): Irochka/123RF; 104 (2): 5 second Studio/Shutterstock; 104 (3): Daniel Vincek/123RF; 104 (4):Tadeusz Wejkszo/123RF; 104 (5): Maria Dryfhout/123RF; 104 (6): Jiang Hongyan/Shutterstock; 104 (7): Geo Martinez/Shutterstock; 104 (8): Sergey Kolesnikov/123RF; 104 (9): Julija Sapic/123RF; 105 (top): Dmitriy Shironosov/123RF; 105 (center): Wavebreak Media Ltd/123RF; 105 (bottom): Iakov Filimonov/123RF; 106: Amble Design/Shutterstock; 107 (cucumber): Daniel Vincek/123RF; 107 (onions): Tadeusz Wejkszo/123RF; 107 (lettuce): Jiang Hongyan/Shutterstock; 107 (peas): Julija Sapic/123RF; 107 (mushroom): Sergey Kolesnikov/123RF; 108 (1): Aneva/123RF; 108 (2): Oleg Vydyborets/123RF; 108 (3): Pushishdonhongsa/123RF; 108 (4): Paulo Leandro Souza de Vilela Pinto/123RF; 108 (5): Bryljaev/123RF; 108 (6): LianeM/Shutterstock; 108 (7): Provasilich/Shutterstock; 108 (8): Viktar Malyshchyts/123RF; 108 (9): Karramba Production/Shutterstock; 109: Sjenner13/Shutterstock; 112 (bread): V.S.Anandhakrishna/Shutterstock; 112 (eggs): Stable/Shutterstock; 112 (chicken): Jiang Hongyan/Shutterstock; 112 (soup): Martin Bech/123RF; 112 (corn flakes): George Tsartsianidis/123RF; 112 (bananas): Viktar Malyshchyts/Shutterstock; 113 (top, left): Duplass/Shutterstock; 113 (top, right): Atic12/Shutterstock; 113 (bottom, right): Blend Images/Shutterstock; 113 (bottom, left): Paulaphoto/Shutterstock; 114 (tuna sandwich): Gilberto Mevi/123RF; 114 (chicken sandwich): Liv Friis-larsen/Shutterstock; 114 (cheeseburger):

Foodandmore/123RF; 114 (baked potato): Olena Danileiko/123RF; 114 (green salad): Rafalstachura/123RF; 114 (fruit salad): Nataliia Kravchuk/123RF; 114 (french fries): Noophoto/Shutterstock; 114 (rice): MaraZe/Shutterstock; 114 (pancake): Hurst Photo/Shutterstock; 114 (eggs and toast): Belchonock/123RF; 114 (cereal): Jennifer Barrow/123RF; 114 (iced tea): Brent Hofacker/123RF; 114 (juice): VictoriaKh/Shutterstock; 114 (coffee): Pikselstock/Shutterstock; 114 (tea): Denis Larkin/Shutterstock; 119: Monticello/Shutterstock.

## Unit 7
Page 123: Cathy Yeulet/123RF; 125: Primagefactory/123RF; 126 (sunny): Alexandre Zveiger/123RF; 126 (new): David Ronald Head/123RF; 126 (large): Katarzyna Bialasiewicz/123RF; 126 (small): Breadmaker/123RF; 128 (top, left): Trevorhirst/E+/Getty Images; 128 (top, center): Iriana88w/123RF; 128 (top, right): Glenn Young/Shutterstock; 128 (bottom, left): Interior Design/Shutterstock; 128 (bottom, center): Artazum/Shutterstock; 128 (bottom, right): Iriana88w/123RF; 131: Wavebreak Media Ltd/123RF; 137: Artazum/Shutterstock.

## Unit 8
Page 141: TZIDO SUN/Shutterstock; 142 (1): Vetasster/Shutterstock; 142 (2): Karkas/Shutterstock; 142 (3): Tarzhanova/123RF; 142 (4): Windu/123RF; 142 (5): Nadezda Tsepaeva/123RF; 142 (6): Ruslan Kudrin/Shutterstock; 142 (7): Karkas/Shutterstock; 142 (8): Olga Popova/Shutterstock; 142(9): Evikka/Shutterstock; 142 (10): Elnur/Shutterstock; 142 (11): Denis Rozhnovsky/Shutterstock; 143 (top, right): Mangostar/123RF; 143 (maxi dress): Tarzhanova/123RF; 143 (sneakers): Denis Rozhnovsky/Shutterstock; 143 (blue sweater): Ruslan Kudrin/Shutterstock; 143 (brown pants): Olga Popova/Shutterstock; 143 (grey skirt): Karkas/Shutterstock; 143 (jeans): Karkas/Shutterstock; 144 (center, right): Dmitry Kalinovsky/123RF; 144(t-shirt): Vetasster/Shutterstock; 144 (socks): Tarzhanova/Shutterstock; 144 (shirt): Nadezda Tsepaeva/123RF; 144 (skirt): Karkas/Shutterstock; 144 (sweater): Ruslan Kudrin/Shutterstock; 144 (jeans): Karkas/Shutterstock; 150 (shirt): Karkas/Shutterstock; 150 (shoes): Heinteh/123RF; 150 (skirt): Karkas/Shutterstock; 150 (jeans): Elnur/Shutterstock; 150 (sweater): Karkas/Shutterstock; 150 (red jacket): Elenovsky/Shutterstock; 151 (sweater): Karina Bakalyan/Shutterstock; 151 (pants): Olga Popova/Shutterstock; 151 (grey t-shirt): Surrphoto/Shutterstock; 151 (shoes): Elnur/Shutterstock; 151 (sneakers): Nataliia Kravchuk/123RF; 151 (hooded jacket): Olga Popova/Shutterstock; 156 (Jane): Maridav/Shutterstock; 156 (Vic): Wong Yu Liang/123RF; 156 (Tara): Jose Manuel Gelpi Diaz/123RF; 156 (Ken): Mark LaMoyne/Shutterstock; 156 (Amy): Javi_Indy/Shutterstock; 158 (Dress): Tarzhanova/Shutterstock; 158 (Jacket): Karkas/Shutterstock; 158 (skirt): Tarzhanova/Shutterstock; 158 (shoes): Heinteh/123RF; 158 (jeans): Elnur/Shutterstock; 158 (sneakers): Denis Rozhnovsky/Shutterstock.

## Unit 9
Page 159: Thinkstock Images/Stockbyte/Getty Images; 160 (go online): Coleman Yuen/Pearson Education Asia Ltd; 160 (play the guitar): Hongqi Zhang/123RF; 160 (listen to music): Takayuki/Shutterstock; 160 ( play soccer): Cathy Yeulet/123RF; 160 (exercise): Robert Kneschke/Shutterstock; 160 (watch TV): Prod-akszyn/Shutterstock; 160 (visit friends): Ferli/123RF; 160 (go to movies): Syda Productions/Shutterstock; 160 (play video games): Shutterstock; 161: Alessio Ponti/Shutterstock; 162 (left):Visuals Stock/Alamy Stock Photo; 162 (right): Oliveromg/Shutterstock; 163 (exercise): Pearson Education Australia Pty Ltd ; 163 (listen to music): Dolgachov/123RF; 163 (watch tv): Sirtravelalot/Shutterstock; 163(play soccer): Wavebreak Media Ltd/123RF; 164 (walk the dog): Moodboard/123RF; 164 (pay bills): Rocketclips, Inc./Shutterstock; 164 (talk on the phone): Shutterstock; 164 (do homework): Adrin Shamsudin/Shutterstock; 164 (wash the car): Volkovslava/Shutterstock; 164 (feed the cat): Littlekidmoment/Shutterstock; 166 (work on the computer): Burlingham/Shutterstock; 166 (help a customer): Dmitry Kalinovsky/123RF; 166 (take a break): Belchonock/123RF; 166 (take orders): Auremar/123RF; 166 (count money): Maryna Pleshkun/123RF; 166 (look for something): Wavebreak Media Ltd/123RF; 166 (answer the phone): Shutterstock; 166 (drive a truck): Robert Carner/123RF; 166 (fix cars): Antoniodiaz/Shutterstock; 167 (truck driver): Robert Carner/123RF; 167 (man counting money): Pisit.Namtasaeng.PS/Shutterstock; 167 (co-workers talking): Wavebreak Media Ltd/123RF; 167 (woman on phone): Dragon Images/Shutterstock; 168 (I'm late for work): Tidty/123RF; 168 (I'm sick): Auremar/123RF; 168 (I can't come to work today): Iakov Filimonov/123RF; 168 (bottom): Tele52/Shutterstock; 169: Tele52/Shutterstock; 173: Wavebreak Media Ltd/123RF; 174 (1): Siriphong Thumpharak/123RF; 174 (2): Andrey Kekyalyaynen/123RF; 174 (3): Wang Tom/123RF; 174 (4): Dragan Grkic/123RF; 174 (5): Sima Hui/123RF; 174 (6): Dolgachov/123RF; 176: Tele52/Shutterstock.

## Unit 10
Page 177: Michaelpuche/Shutterstock; 178 (1): Hiya Images/Corbis/Getty Images; 178 (2): LEDOMSTOCK/Shutterstock; 178 (3): Daniil Peshkov/123RF; 178 (4): Shutterstock; 178 (5): Sandsun/Shutterstock; 178 (6): V J Matthew/Shutterstock; 178 (7): 06photo/Shutterstock; 178 (8): MIXA/SOURCENEXT/Alamy Stock Photo; 178 (9): Wizdata/Shutterstock; 180 (1): David R. Frazier/Danita Delimont Photography/Newscom; 180 (2): Glen Jones/Shutterstock; 180 (3): Ken Wolter/Shutterstock; 180 (4): Lim Yong Hian/Shutterstock; 180 (5): Bildagentur Zoonar GmbH/Shutterstock; 180 (6): Patrick baehl de Lescure/Shutterstock; 180 (7): Steve Heap/Shutterstock; 180 (8): Ellen Clark/Alamy Stock Photo; 180 (9): Cathy Yeulet/Shutterstock; 182 (1): BraunS/E+/Getty Images; 182 (2): Martin Novak/Shutterstock; 182 (3): Tetra Images/Getty Images; 182 (4): Dean Drobot/123RF; 182 (5): Maskot/Getty Images; 182 (6): Luciano Leon/Alamy Stock Photo; 182 (7): Kristi Blokhin/Shutterstock; 182 (8): Leezsnow/iStock/Getty Images; 182 (9): Patti McConville/Alamy Stock Photo; 183: Apeloga AB/Cultura/Getty Images; 185: Iakov Filimonov/123RF; 186 (1): Sue Smith/Shutterstock; 186 (2): Robert J. Beyers II/Shutterstock; 186 (3, left): Steve Hamblin/Alamy Stock Photo; 186 (3, right): Steve Hamblin/Alamy Stock Photo; 186 (4): Creative icon styles/Shutterstock; 186(5): Georgios Kollidas/Shutterstock; 186 (6): Robert J. Beyers II/Shutterstock; 186 (7): Sue Smith/Shutterstock; 186 (8): Hank Shiffman/Shutterstock; 187 (stop sign): Sue Smith/Shutterstock; 187 (do not enter): Creative icon styles/Shutterstock; 187 (no parking): Georgios Kollidas/Shutterstock; 187 (speed limit 25): Hank Shiffman/Shutterstock; 187 (no u-turn): Robert J. Beyers II/Shutterstock; 187 (one way): Sue Smith/Shutterstock; 187 (no u-turn): Robert J. Beyers II/Shutterstock; 187 (walk): Steve Hamblin/Alamy Stock Photo; 187(don't walk): Steve Hamblin/Alamy Stock Photo; 187 (no parking): Georgios Kollidas/Shutterstock; 187 (stop): Sue Smith/Shutterstock; 187 (do not enter): Creative icon styles/Shutterstock; 187 (speed limit 25): Hank Shiffman/Shutterstock; 191 (1): Maskot/Getty Images; 191 (2): Allen.G/Shutterstock; 191 (3): Hugo Felix/123RF; 191 (4): Belchonock/123RF; 191 (5): BraunS/E+/Getty Images; 191 (6): Tommaso Altamura/123RF; 191 (7): Sheila Fitzgerald/Shutterstock; 191 (8): Leezsnow/iStock/Getty Images; 194 (1): SHUBIN.INFO/Shutterstock; 194 (2): PaylessImages/123RF; 194 (3): Janifest/123RF; 194 (4): Maximkabb/123RF; 94 (5): Alexander Oganezov/Shutterstock; 194 (6): Micha Weber/Shutterstock.

## Unit 11
Page 195: Shutterstock; 196 (left): Ebtikar/Shutterstock; 196 (right): Ebtikar/Shutterstock; 197 (left): Belchonock/123RF; 197 (right): Manuel Faba Ortega/123RF; 199: Shutterstock; 201 (top, left): Nattanit Pumpuang/123RF; 201 (top, right): Subbotina Anna/Shutterstock; 201 (bottom, left): James Steidl/Shutterstock; 201 (bottom, right): MBI/Shutterstock; 209 (1): Viacheslav Iakobchuk/123RF; 209 (2): Mangostock/Shutterstock; 209 (3): Kurhan/Shutterstock; 211: Subbotina Anna/Shutterstock.

## Unit 12
Page 213: Kali9/E+/Getty Images; 214 (1): Michaeljung/Shutterstock; 214 (2): Shutterstock; 214 (3): Michaeljung/Shutterstock; 214 (4): Steve Debenport/E+/Getty Images; 214 (5): Graham Oliver/123RF; 214 (6): Michaeljung/Shutterstock; 214 (7): Hongqi Zhang/123RF; 214 (8): Dean Drobot/Shutterstock; 214 (9): Dolgachov/123RF; 215: William Perugini/123RF; 216 (1): Odua Images/Shutterstock ; 216 (2): PT Images/Shutterstock; 216 (3): Dmitry Kalinovsky/123RF; 216 (4): Hill Street Studios/DigitalVision/Getty Images; 216 (5): Rob Marmion/Shutterstock; 216 (6): Steven Vona/Shutterstock; 216 (7): PaylessImages/123RF; 216 (8): Nakamasa/Shutterstock; 216 (9): Andrey_Popov/Shutterstock; 218 (1): Koh sze kiat/Shutterstock; 218 (2): Jens Brüggemann/123RF; 218 (3): Ferli/123RF; 218 (4): Lucky Business/Shutterstock; 218 (5): Chutima Chaochaiya/Shutterstock; 218 (6): Sue Smith/Shutterstock; 218 (7): Andriy Popov/Shutterstock; 218 (8): Dmitry Kalinovsky/Shutterstock; 218 (9): Cathy Yeulet/123RF; 219: Stockfour/Shutterstock; 220: Konstantin Pelikh/Shutterstock; 222 (1): Petervick167/123RF; 222 (2): Dzhafarov Eduard/Shutterstock; 222 (3): Vadim Guzhva/123RF; 222 (4): Michaeljung/Shutterstock; 222 (5): LightField Studios/Shutterstock; 222 (6): Scott Griessel/123RF.

**Illustrations:** Luis Briseno, pp. 130; Laurie Conley, pp. 33, 113, 147 (bottom), 148 (top), 149 (bottom), 155 (bottom), 198; Deborah Crowle, pp. 6; Len Ebert represented by Ann Remen-Willis, pp. 16, 68, 86, 129, 148 (bottom); ElectraGraphics, pp. 18, 19, 22, 26, 37, 42, 46, 48, 49, 50, 60, 63-64, 76, 77, 80, 84, 94, 95, 98, 102, 110 (bottom), 118, 122, 124, 136, 146, 154, 172, 179, 181, 184, 185, 186 (#2, 4, 5, 6, 7, 8, 9), 188, 190, 192, 193, 202, 203, 208, 212, 226, 230; Peter Grau, pp. 20, 40, 58, 78, 96, 116, 134, 152, 170, 206, 224; Brian Hughes, pp. 110 (top), 111, 112, 144, 204; Luis Montiel, pp. 175; Roberto Sadi, pp. 34-35, 45, 125, 126, 139, 155 (top), 157; Neil Stewart/NSV Productions, pp. 72, 205; Meryl Treatner, pp. 147 (top), 164; Anna Veltfort, pp. 30, 36, 145, 149 (top), 200